The History of

Al-Khilafah
Ar-Rashidah

Upper Elementry/Junior Level

Dr. 'Abdullah al-Ahsan

Illustrations by
Jennifer Mazzoni

IQRA' International Educational Foundation Chicago

Part of a Comprehensive and Systematic Program of Islamic Studies

A Textbook for
Islamic Social Studies
Upper Elementary/Junior Level

The History of
Al-Khilafah Ar-Rashidah

Chief Program Editors
Dr. Abidullah al-Ansari Ghazi
(Ph.D., History of Religion
 Harvard University)

Tasneema K. Ghazi
(Ph.D., Curriculum-Reading
 University of Minnesota)

Reviewed by
Dr. Robert N. Delk
(Ph. D., Univesity of Madison)

Dr. Ghulam Haider Aasi
(Ph. D., Temple University)

Fadel Abdallah
(M.A. Arabic, Islamic Studies,
University of Minnesota)

Language Editing
Noura Durkee
(M.A. Fine Arts, Princeton)

Huseyin Abiva
(B.A. History, University of Maryland)

Designer
Aliuddin Khaja
Civil Engineering
India

Map Illustrations
Huseyin Abiva
(B.A. History, University of Maryland)

Jennifer Mazzoni
(B.A. Illustration,
Columbia College Chicago)

Illustrations
Jennifer Mazzoni
(B.A. Illustration,
Columbia College Chicago)

Second printing April, 2001
Printed by Elite Publishers Ltd. Pakistan

Special note on copyright:
This book is a part of IQRA's comprehensive
and systematic program of Islamic Studies
being developed for Islamic Education.

No part of this book may be reproduced by
any means including photocopying, electronic,
mechanical, recording, or otherwise without
the written consent of the publisher. In specific
cases, permission is granted on written request
to publish or translate IQRA's works. For
information regarding permission, write to:
**IQRA' International Educational Foundation,
7450 Skokie Blvd., Skokie, IL 60077
Tel: 847-673-4072
Fax : 847-673-4095**

Library of Congress Catalog Card Number 94-75416
ISBN # 1-56316-366-7

Printed by
Ⓔ Elite Publishers Ltd.
D-118, S.I.T.E.,
Karachi-75700 Pakistan
Tel:2573435 - 5, 2579536
E-mail: elite@elite.com.pk

Contents

Dedicated to

Hafsa, Saeb, Arqam,

and

all Muslim children

Acknowledgements

Literary Grant 1993
FAITH FOUNDATION
(Foundation of American Islamic
Teaching and Heritage)
for publication of this textbook

The Words of Rasulullah ﷺ Concerning Al Khulafa' Ar-Rashidun

The Prophet Muhammad ﷺ left us with many of his words describing and confirming the high virtues of his *Sahabah* (*Radiya Allahu Ta'ala 'an-hum*) and more specially of *al-Khulafa' ar-Rashidun,* 'Abu Bakr, 'Umar, 'Uthman and 'Ali ﷺ. Through these various *ahadith* we can see the love and respect that Rasulullah (*Salla-Allahu 'alaihi wa sallam*) had for them.

Rasulullah ﷺ said:

- About his *Sahabah* ﷺ:
  My companions are like guiding stars; whomever you follow, you will be rightly guided.

- About 'Abu Bakr ﷺ:
  Never had I presented Islam to any one who had not stumbled (reluctant at first); except 'Abu Bakr ﷺ, he did not hesitate.

- About 'Umar ﷺ:
  Verily (surely) Allah has placed the truth on the tongue of 'Umar and in his heart. I have never seen a genius who is as decisive as he is (in regard to truth).

- About 'Uthman ﷺ:
  O Allah! Be satisfied with Uthman for I am satisfied with him.

- About 'Ali ﷺ:
  Whoever has me as his friend and protector also has 'Ali as his friend and protector.

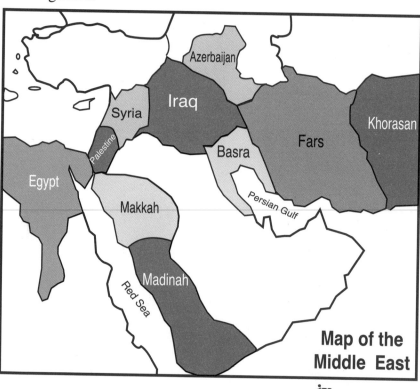

Map of the Middle East

Azerbaijan
Iraq
Syria
Khorasan
Palestine
Fars
Basra
Egypt
Persian Gulf
Makkah
Madinah
Red Sea

IQRA's Note for Parents and Teachers

This textbook, The History of *Al-Khilafah Ar-Rashidah* (Upper Elementary/Junior Level), with accompanying workbook, is part of IQRA's comprehensive and System-atic Program of Social Studies.

Islamic History is an important subject which must be taught to our children and youth from an early age. *Al-Khilafah Ar-Rashidah* (The Rightly Guided Caliphate) is the most important period in Islamic history; following the Prophet's *Sunnah*, it established the principle of *Shura* (consultation), responsible government, rule of law, a welfare system, and human rights. The early *Khilafah* represented Islamic values and provided guarantees of human rights for all. *Al-Khilafah Ar-Rashidah* represents those norms of Islamic government that later became an ideal for all Islamic governments and its officials to follow.

The companion workbook, written by a young educator, Nilofer Abiva, offers important exercises providing reinforcement of reading and helps the child to develop the skills of problem solving, sequencing, drawing inferences, evaluating, analyzing, and synthesizing. Workbooks are an essential part of IQRA's educational program and must be used to gain the best results in creative teaching. Teachers are strongly urged to use the textbooks with the workbooks to have the best results and to make teaching and learning a challenge and fun.

IQRA' is also publishing a companion en-rich-ment book, The Stories of *Al-Khulafa' Ar-Rashidun* (at levels elementary/junior) by Huseyin Abiva. This book can be used to learn about inspiring stories from the lives of the Rightly Guided Caliphs. This enrichment book tells inspiring stories of faith, love, sacrifice, and wisdom of these very special *Sahabah* of Rasulullah .

IQRA' is also developing a comprehensive work on Islamic history at the Senior level, of which the first volume will be ready by Fall 2001, *Insha Allah*. In view of the great importance of Islamic culture and spiritual heritage, IQRA' has undertaken an extensive program to publish a series on the life of *Sahabah* , *At-Tabi'un* (the generation that followed the *Sahabah)*, *As-Salaf As-Salih* (the Pious Ances-tors) and other important personalities in Islamic history. It is also publishing a series of Islamic stories and anecdotes to enrich the reading for young Muslims and provide them true Islamic role models.

> ### EDITORIAL NOTE
>
> Based on the opinion of some of the book reviewers, it should be noted that, occasionally, the lengthy quotations in this book are free and liberal interpretations by the author, varying from the original Arabic language. This was dictated by the need to simplify the language (as well as the situations) to make it easier for the children to understand.

بسم الله الرحمن الرحيم

لَقَدْ جَآءَكُمْ رَسُولٌ مِّنْ
أَنفُسِكُمْ عَزِيزٌ عَلَيْهِ مَا عَنِتُّمْ حَرِيصٌ
عَلَيْكُم بِالْمُؤْمِنِينَ رَءُوفٌ رَّحِيمٌ

*"There has come to you a Messenger
from among you, it grieves him that you
are overburdened,
full of concern for you, for the Believers
he is most gentle
and full of kindness."*

(At-Tawbah 9:128)

Introduction

Allah, our Creator, sent us a blessed Messenger 🕌 to bring us His Book and to show, by his life, the best way for us to live. In the preceding Qur'anic passage we read five things about our Messenger, Rasulullah 🕌:

1. He came from among ourselves.

2. Our sufferings grieve him.

3. He is concerned for us.

4. He is most gentle to the believers.

5. He is full of kindness.

These characteristics made the *Sahabah* 🕌 love the Prophet 🕌 and draw closer to him. Some people gave up everything they had because they believed that his teachings and examples would lead them to the best of this world and the best of the Hereafter. When asked to leave their homes and families in Makkah and migrate to Madinah they readily did so. They moved to a new city to live among the strangers with whom they were united in faith to build a new society. These are the people we call the *Saha-bah* of the Prophet 🕌, his Companions. By being close to him most of the time, his *Sahabah* 🕌 took on some of his noble characteristics

You have noted that two Arabic terms have been mentioned in this discussion. One is the term *'Ummah* and the other is *Al-Khulafa' Ar-Rashidun*. The term *'Ummah* means community or people. But *'Ummah* means much more than community or people. This term has been mentioned in the Qur'an and followers of Rasulullah 🕌 have been mentioned as *Khairu 'Ummah* (the Best Community).

The word *Khulafa'* is the plural form of the Arabic word *Khalifah* or caliph. *Khalifah* means successor or vicegerent 'Abu Bakr As-Siddiq 🕌 succeeded the Prophet 🕌 as the leader of the *'Ummah* and adopted this title. The first four *Khulafa'* ruled for about thirty years. They followed Islamic teachings in every aspect of their personal and public lives. Therefore, they are known as the *Rashidun* or Rightly-Guided. The Muslim historians do not consider the rule of most of the later *Khulafa'* as being rightly-guided. (The other *Khulafa'* did many good works but they also occasionally deviated from some of the teachings of Islam.)

In the following pages, we shall describe some of the activities of the first four *Khulafa'* which illustrate their Islamic characters and their surrender to Allah and love for His Prophet 🕌.

and became like him, compassionate and concerned for other believers. They took others' sufferings upon themselves and they gave themselves to the service of Allah ﷻ, His Prophet ﷺ and His people. Rasulullah ﷺ himself said about them,

> "My Companions are like guiding stars. Whomever you follow, you will be rightly guided."

In this book, *Insha' Allah*, we shall relate the stories of the lives of the four of the closest *Sahabah* of Rasulullah ﷺ: 'Abu Bakr As-Siddiq, 'Umar ibn Al-Khattab, 'Uthman Ibn 'Affan and 'Ali Ibn 'Abi Talib, ﷺ (May Allah be pleased with them). These four *Sahabah* ﷺ stayed very close to Rasulullah ﷺ throughout his life, learning his ways of worship, of guiding people, of inviting people to Islam, and of governing. They worked with him, prayed with him and made *Jihad* along with him. They took guidance from his *Sunnah* and they were able to pass it on to other people. After the demise of Rasulullah ﷺ from this life, these four men succeeded him one after the other in leading the Islamic community, the *'Ummah*. Collectively, they are known as the *Al-Khulafa' Ar-Rashidun*, the Rightly Guided Caliphs.

Words and Terms to Remember:

1. *Sahabah (sing. Sahabi):*
   The Companions. *Sahabah* more specifically means the Companions of the Prophet ﷺ. *Sahabi* took the *Shahadah* in the life of Rasulullah ﷺ and saw him, at least once.

2. *'Ummah:*
   The community. The word *'Ummah* more specifically means the Muslim community.

3. *Khalifah (pl. Khulafa'):*
   The caliph or successor. A title for the leader of the Muslim community.

4. *Ar-Rashidun:*
   The rightly guided. This term is used for the first four *Khulafa'* of Islam.

5. *Deviate:*
   To move away from the original meaning or practice.

We Have Learned:

- Rasulullah ﷺ established the Muslim *'Ummah* and trained and prepared a number of individuals to lead the *'Ummah* after him.

- The four leaders of Islam following Rasulullah ﷺ are known as *Al-Khulafa' Ar-Rashidun*.

- The rule of *Al-Khulafa' Ar-Rashidun* continued for about thirty years.

The Passing of Rasulullah ﷺ

Some time had passed after the Farewell Pil-grimage. Allah ﷻ declared in His Glorious Qur'an that His Guidance was complete. He said:

"Today I have completed your *din* for you."
(Al-Ma'idah, 5:3)

The Revelation of Allah was finally completed in the Qur'an. The religion of Islam as *Ad-Din,* a complete way of life, was revealed and Rasulullah ﷺ has hown through his *Sunnah,* the example, how to practice Islam. Rasulullah ﷺ during his Farewell Sermon on his last pilgrimage, making his *'Ummah* a witness to his work, asked those who were present there:

"Do you bear witness that I have conveyed the message of Islam to you ?" "Yes, O Rasulullah!" answered the crowd. The Prophet ﷺ again asked,

"Will you then convey this message to those who are not present here?"

"We accept the responsibility, O Rasulullah !" replied the crowd.

Thus Rasulullah ﷺ saw to it that his *'Ummah* continued to teach the message of Islam for all times to come. This Farewell Pilgrimage was a signal to many among the *Sahabah* that the mission of Rasulullah ﷺ was now completed and he may leave this world soon.

Many leading companions were grieved by this thought. They could not bear the thought of losing Rasulullah ﷺ, whom they loved so much. They also understood

---

Portions of the Farewell Sermon of Rasulullah ﷺ

All praise be to Allah. We glorify Him and we ask for His help and forgiveness. O People! Listen to me, for I do not know if I will be with you after this year. O Muslims, your blood, property, and honor are sacred and protected until you appear before your Lord. Surely you will meet your Lord and be answerable for all of your actions. Beware, only the one who has committed a crime is responsible for it.

Listen to my words and understand them, Know that a Muslim is the brother of every Muslim and they form one *'Ummah*. I have left among you the Book of Allah and the example of His Messenger.

that the responsibility of spreading the message was now going to fall on the followers of the Rasulullah ﷺ. They knew that Allah's Book (the Qur'an) and Rasulullah's *Sunnah* (way of life) would always be a guide for them and for the *'Ummah* for all time to come. Soon after the Farewell Pilgrimage Rasulullah ﷺ fell ill. Everybody was worried. The thought of Rasulullah ﷺ ever leaving them grieved them very much. How could they live without him? Who would counsel them at difficult times, and with whom would they share their happy moments? Who would lead the regular pray-ers? Rasulullah ﷺ was aware of all these concerns of his *Sahabah*. He instructed his close friend, 'Abu Bakr ﷺ, who had accompanied him during the difficult path of *Hijrah* from Makkah to Madinah, to lead regular prayers during his sickness. To many Muslims, this was an indication that he was to succeed Rasulullah ﷺ in leading the *'Ummah*. However, Rasulullah ﷺ did not specifically mention who was to succeed him.

Rasulullah ﷺ suffered from illness for some days and then passed on to the next life. The followers were so overwhelmed with sorrow that some of them did not want to believe that he could die. 'Umar ﷺ, because of his great love for Rasulullah ﷺ, lost control over his emotions and stood up before the people gathered at Rasulullah's door and insisted that the Prophet ﷺ was not dead and that he would return. While he was talking, 'Abu Bakr ﷺ came and went to the house of 'A'ishah ﷺ where the body of Rasulullah ﷺ was lying. There he said farewell to Rasulullah ﷺ. Then he came out and spoke to the people, saying,

> "Oh people, if anyone worships Muhammad know that Muhammad is dead; if anyone worships Allah, know that Allah is Alive and He never dies."

And then he recited this verse from the Holy Qur'an,

> "Muhammad is nothing but a messenger. Messengers have passed away before him. Can it be that if he were to die or be killed you would turn back on your heels? He who turns back does no harm to Allah and Allah will reward the grateful." (*'Al 'Imran 3:144*)

Although that verse had been revealed at the Battle of *'Uhud* (3rd year of *Hijrah*), when the Prophet ﷺ was wounded, it was as if the people had never heard it before. 'Umar ﷺ said later that when he heard that verse from 'Abu Bakr ﷺ he fell to the ground, knowing for sure that the Prophet ﷺ was indeed dead. All Muslims accepted the fact of Rasulullah's death. His demise was on the 12th of *Rabi' 'Al-'Awwal*, 11th *Hijrah* year (June 8th, 632 C.E.).

4

Words and Terms to Remember:

1. *'Ad-Din:*
   The way of life or religion. For Muslims *Din* means Allah's complete guidance for our lives.

2. *Farewell pilgrimage:*
   The last pilgrimage of Rasulullah ﷺ before his death.

3. *Hijrah:*
   The migration of Rasulullah ﷺ and his *Sahabah* from Makkah to Madinah.

4. *Sunnah:*
   The sayings and practices of Rasulullah ﷺ.

5. *Rabi' 'Al-Awwal:*
   The third month of the Islamic Calendar.

We Have Learned:

- At the Farewell Pilgrimage, Allah ﷻ revealed that the Message of Islam was completed for all times.

- Rasulullah ﷺ left no clear instruction about his succession, but he asked 'Abu Bakr ﱠ to lead prayers during his illness.

- 'Abu Bakr ﱠ reminded people that the Message of the Qur'an is that Allah ﷻ is Eternal and anyone who is born will die one day.

'Abu Bakr ⚬ Becomes the Khalifah

As soon as the news about the death of Rasulullah ⚬ spread, Muslims became extremely shocked and worried. They were shocked because they loved him very much; they were worried about the future of the Muslim 'Ummah now that there was no leader. After the death of Rasulullah ⚬, they knew that the Guidance to mankind was completed and they had the responsi-bility to carry on the Message.

Some 'Ansar, the original inhabitants of Madinah, who helped Rasulullah ⚬ in establishing the 'Ummah, got together at the Council Hall of Banu Sa'idah. The Banu Sa'idah was one of the original tribes of Madinah. When 'Abu Bakr ⚬ and 'Umar ⚬ heard about the gathering, they went quickly to it, fearing a decision that might cause confusion and division in the 'Ummah. In the meantime, some other leaders of the Muhajirun and Quraish arrived there also. They found everyone discussing the succession to Rasulullah ⚬. Some of the 'Ansar said,

> "The new leader should come from among us. We are the original inhabitants of Madinah and we protected Rasulullah ⚬ and offered him refuge."

Others from Makkah argued,

> "Only a member of the Quraish deserves to be the leader of the 'Ummah; they were first to accept Islam; they have suffered and sacrificed most for the sake of Islam."

It seems there was going to be a terrible division in the 'Ummah. 'Abu Bakr ⚬ got up and said,

> "All the good things that the 'Ansar have said about themselves are well deserved. But the Arabs will recognize the authority only of the clan of the Quraish. I offer you one of the two men; accept either of them as you please."

He then took the hands of 'Umar ⚬ and Abu 'Ubaidah ibn Al-Jarrah ⚬ and offered those to the people for the bai'ah, the pledge to obey.

But the people did not accept this. One of the 'Ansar then suggested that let there be two leaders, one from the Muhajirun and one from the 'Ansar. Others reacted sharply to this proposal, saying it would divide the 'Ummah. 'Umar ⚬ suddenly said,

> "O 'Abu Bakr, how can anyone else fill this

office as long as you are alive? You are the most prominent of the *Muhajirun.* You were the companion of Rasulullah in the cave of Thawr. You led the *Salah* during the last days of his life. Hold out your hand so that I may give my allegiance to you!"

'Umar took the initiative, gave him the *bai'ah* (allegiance) by taking his hand in his own hand and pledging his loyalty. The people gathered in the hall and realized the wisdom of 'Umar's words and action and followed him in giving the *bai'ah.* Many of them then realized that, in fact, the Prophet had himself given many signs that 'Abu Bakr was his own choice.

The next day, 'Abu Bakr sat before the people in the *Masjid* to take general *bai'ah.* 'Umar got up first and said,

"O people, yesterday I said something which I do not find in Allah's Book nor was it something which Rasulullah entrusted to me; but I thought that Rasulullah would order our affairs until he was the last of us alive. This is why I could not believe he had died. Allah has left His Book with you, by which He guided His Prophet and if you hold fast to that, Allah will guide you as He guided the Prophet. Allah has placed your affairs in the hands of the best one among you, the companion of the Prophet, the second of the two when they were in the cave, so arise and pledge allegiance to him."

This all the people of Madinah did, except 'Ali, who did so later. 'Abu Bakr rose, praised Allah and said,

"O Muslims! I have been given authority over you and I am not the best of you. If I do well, help me; and if I do wrong, set me right. Loyalty is to tell the truth to a leader; treason is to hide it. The weak among you will be powerful in my eyes until I secure his rights, if Allah so Wills. The strong among you shall be weak in my eyes until I get the right from him. If people do not follow in the way of Allah, He will disgrace them. If people become wicked, Allah will bring punishment on us all. Obey me as long as I obey Allah and His Prophet and if I disobey them you owe me no obedience. Let us now rise for *Salah* and may Allah have Mercy on us all."

This was a very important speech for the formation of the *'Ummah.* In it, 'Abu Bakr defined the rights and responsibilities of a ruler and of subjects. He also indicated one should help a ruler through good advice. 'Abu Bakr also informed the community members of their right to warn and correct the *Khalifah* if he did anything against the teachings of the Qur'an and the example of Rasulullah.

Words and Terms to Remember:

1. *'Ansar (sing. 'Ansari):*
   Helper. This term particularly refers to those inhabitants of Madinah who invited Rasulullah ﷺ to their city, and helped him for the cause of Islam.

2. *Al-Bai'ah:*
   The pledge, allegiance or the declaration of one's willingness to support and obey someone.

3. *Muhajirun (sing. Muhajir):*
   The immigrants. This refers to those Muslims of Makkah who migrated to Madinah along with the Prophet ﷺ.

4. *Treason:*
   To turn against someone who trusted you.

We Have Learned:

- After the death of Rasulullah ﷺ, some Muslims gathered in the Council Hall of Banu Sa'idah to discuss his succession.

- 'Umar ﷺ first proposed and declared his allegiance to 'Abu Bakr as the successor to Rasulullah ﷺ.

- 'Abu Bakr ﷺ requested the Muslims to help him as *Khalifah* of Rasulullah ﷺ by offering him assistance and counsel.

Early Life of Abu Bakr ؓ

'Abu Bakr ؓ belonged to a clan of the famous Quraish tribe of Makkah. He was born in 573 C.E, about three years after the birth of Rasulullah ﷺ. He was a businessman and frequently travelled outside Arabia for business purposes. A number of times he accompanied Rasulullah ﷺ on trading caravans and developed a very intimate friendship with him. He was very close to Rasulullah ﷺ and knew that he was a truthful and a pious man. When Rasulullah ﷺ declared his prophethood, 'Abu Bakr ؓ immediately believed in him and accepted Islam.

On another occasion, when Rasulullah ﷺ disclosed that he was taken by Allah's wish to Jerusalem one night *('Isra')* and then to Heaven *(Mi'raj)* in His presence, most of the people of Makkah did not believe him. Some enemies of Rasulullah ﷺ had even started to say, "Muhammad has gone crazy. He has started to make up stories that he has gone overnight to Jerusalem and then from there to Heaven to meet God Himself. How can anyone believe this?"

When 'Abu Bakr ؓ came to know about this, he said, "If Muhammad says so, I believe it." This disappointed the nonbelievers greatly, but it increased 'Abu Bakr's honor in the sight of Allah and Rasulullah ﷺ tremendously. This unreserved trust of 'Abu Bakr ؓ in the mission of Rasulullah ﷺ earned him the beautiful title *As-Siddiq* or "The Truthful One."

'Abu Bakr ؓ was a moderately rich person. He always contributed to help the poor and support the cause of Islam. During the early days of Islam in Makkah, persecution of Muslims at the hands of non-Muslims was a common practice. Once Bilal ؓ, an Ethiopian slave, was being tortured by his master for accepting Islam. Seeing this, 'Abu Bakr ؓ went to his master and bought Bilal's ؓ freedom, who became a free man. He also paid for the land on which the *Masjid un-Nabi* in Madinah was built.

On the occasion of the battle of *Tabuk* in 9 A.H., Muslims needed a lot of money for a campaign against the powerful Byzantine emperor. Rasulullah ﷺ appealed for generous contributions from every single individual in Madinah. People brought to the Prophet ﷺ whatever they could but 'Abu Bakr ؓ donated everything that he possessed at that time. When Rasulullah ﷺ asked him why he didn't keep something for his family, he replied, "Allah and His Prophet are sufficient for me."

'Abu Bakr's faith was complete. He knew that everything he had came from Allah and to Him it would be returned. Indeed, Allah restored his wealth back to him within a short time, and he continued to give it away with equal generosity.

For 'Abu Bakr Islam was the most important fact of his life. The story is told of his son who at first did not embrace Islam and who fought against the Muslims in various battles. Later, he realized the truth of Islam and accepted it. Once he told his father,

"O father! You came several times within the range of my sword, but I did not kill you."

"I would not have spared you, if you had come within the range of my sword even for a single moment," said 'Abu Bakr in response.

Did this mean that 'Abu Bakr did not love his son? Of course not, he loved his son dearly, but it meant that 'Abu Bakr loved Allah more than his own son. A son who defied Allah and His Prophet and raised sword against Islam could not deserve any love from a person like 'Abu Bakr.

It was extreme love of Rasulullah that made him offer his young and intelligent daughter in marriage to him. 'A'ishah became 'Umm ul-Mu'minin, the Mother of the Believers and a great teacher of the 'Ummah.

'A'ishah, the Daughter of Abu Bakr

One of the most important women in the History of Islam was 'Ummu-l-Mu'minin 'A'ishah the daughter of 'Abu Bakr. At an early age she married Rasulullah and stayed with him until his passing from this life. She learned Islam from Rasulullah and became a teacher in her own right. It is reported that one third of Din is related through her.

Words and Terms to Remember:

1. *'Isra':*
   The nightly journey of Rasulullah ﷺ from *Bait-Allah* to *Bait al-Maqdis* (Jerusalem).

2. *Mi'raj:*
   Prophet's ﷺ night journey from Jerusalem to the Heavens.

3. *'As-Siddiq:*
   "The Truthful One." This name was given to 'Abu Bakr ﷺ by Rasulullah ﷺ for his trusting friendship.

4. *Persecution:*
   When a strong person shows cruelty to someone who is weak.

We Have Learned:

- 'Abu Bakr ﷺ was a businessman and good friend of Rasulullah ﷺ.

- 'Abu Bakr ﷺ was given the title *As-Siddiq* for his trust in Rasulullah ﷺ.

- During the *Tabuk* campaign, 'Abu Bakr ﷺ contributed all the wealth he owned to the cause of Islam.

11

The Immediate Task

The immediate task that 'Abu Bakr ⌘ faced was to make arrangements for the burial of Rasulullah ⌘. Did you realize that the election of 'Abu Bakr ⌘ as the leader of the *Ummah* was completed before the Prophet ⌘ was laid to rest. This tells us the importance of having a leader for the community. This also teaches us about the importance which Islam places on discipline. Without leadership, Muslims could not have achieved such discipline. Therefore, they elected a leader first, and made arrangements for the burial of Rasulullah ⌘ later.

After the body of Rasulullah ⌘ was prepared for burial by 'Ali ⌘ and other close family members, the whole community came to say the funeral prayer beside his body. Then he was buried in 'A'ishah's ⌘ apartment; 'Abu Bakr ⌘ remembered the saying of Rasulullah ⌘, "A Prophet must be buried where he dies."

As soon as the burial was over, 'Abu Bakr ⌘ undertook an unfinished task of the Prophet ⌘. Just before his death, Rasulullah ⌘ had dispatched an army against some tribes in Syria. He wanted to punish the Syrian tribes because they had killed a Muslim ambassador to their leader. This was a major crime according to the rules of diplomacy in those days and in our time as well! Therefore, Rasulullah ⌘ had sent Zaid ibn Harithah ⌘, a *Sahabi* whom he loved like a son, to punish them. But the tribes were under the protection of the Byzantine emperor, and Zaid ⌘ was defeated and martyred in the battle.

Rasulullah ⌘ decided to dispatch another army against the Christian Byzantines.

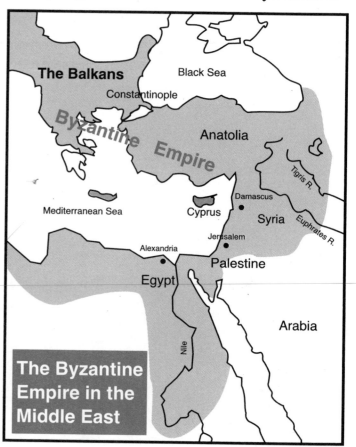

The Byzantine Empire in the Middle East

Rasulullah named 'Usamah, young son of Zaid, to lead this new force. The Prophet had known 'Usamah since birth and had great confidence in him in spite of his young age. However, the Prophet died while the preparation was being made for this campaign.

'Abu Bakr decided to undertake this unfinished task of Rasulullah. He ordered the departure of the army against the Byzantines. Originally, the Prophet had asked 'Abu Bakr also to accompany 'Usamah to Syria. Under the new circumstances, 'Abu Bakr, as the new *Khalifah* of the *'Ummah* could not leave Madinah. Therefore, he had requested 'Usamah's permission to stay behind in Madinah. Usamah granted the request out of respect. Do you know how old Usamah was at that time? He was only nineteen years old, and famous generals like Khalid ibn Al-Walid were placed under his command.

As the army was ready to leave, 'Abu Bakr held the reigns of the horse of 'Usamah in his hands and walked the horse to the outskirts of the city. 'Usamah, the young commander, sat on the horse as 'Abu Bakr walked on foot. 'Usamah felt em-barrassed as 'Abu Bakr told him,

> "You are the commander of the Muslim army. You were appointed by Rasulullah for this campaign. You are our leader now."

As they reached the departure point, 'Abu Bakr advised 'Usamah about his responsibility as a leader and about the code of conduct for an Islamic army:

> "Be careful against any wrong act. Don't kill any child, woman, or old people. Don't destroy any plant or tree that provides food to human beings or animals. Do not kill animals unless they are needed for food and sustenance. You may eat meat and other food supplied to you by the local population by pronouncing the name of Allah over it. Don't persecute the peace loving Christian monks and priests. March forward in the name of Allah and may He protect you."

'Usamah left Madinah for Syria in the 11th year of *Hijrah* (632 C.E.). When 'Usamah engaged the enemy, he first sought those individuals who were responsible for the killing of his father, Zaid. The Byzantine forces in the area avoided confrontation with the Muslims, there was no battle, but 'Usamah captured the culprits and punished them. The local tribes offered their allegiance to the *Khalifah* in Madinah. Muslims achieved victory in their mission, and bloodshed was avoided.

A Bedouin woman with her son

13

Words and Terms to Remember:

1. *Byzantine Empire:*
   The Eastern Roman Empire with Constantinople (modern-day Istanbul) as their capital city.

2. *Sustenance:*
   What humans need to survive, such as food and shelter.

3. *Campaign:*
   When an army moves against its enemies and fights a series of battles.

We Have Learned:

- 'Abu Bakr ﷺ was elected *Khalifah* even before the burial of Rasulullah ﷺ.

- Young 'Usamah ﷺ led the Muslim campaign against Syria.

- 'Abu Bakr ﷺ asked the Muslim army to respect the life and safety of children, women, old people, plants and animals.

The Revolt of Tribes

In pre-Islamic Arabia (which was known as *Jahiliyyah,* the Age of Ignorance), people were divided into tribes and clans. They used to fight frequently against each other. They also used to make defense agreements with stronger tribes. *Quraish,* the Prophet's ﷺ tribe, was one of the strongest tribes in pre-Islamic Arabia. When Rasulullah ﷺ established the 'Ummah and the pagans of *Quraish* were defeated, almost all tribes of Arabia joined the Muslim 'Ummah. However, after the death of the Prophet ﷺ, some tribes revolted and tried to divide the 'Ummah and 'Abu Bakr ﷺ had to deal with this difficult situation.

When 'Usamah ibn Zaid ﷺ left Madinah for Syria, several tribes of Arabia revolted against Islam and attacked Madinah itself. This was a major threat to the existence of the 'Ummah. These tribes had been unruly during the pre-Islamic period. In fact because of their unruly and indisciplined behavior and their lack of belief, Muslims described this period of history as *Jahiliyyah* or the Age of Ignorance.

We have learned that 'Abu Bakr ﷺ was originally elected by a selected group of individuals in Madinah. The rest of the people of Madinah quickly declared their allegiance to him as well. In those days, it was not possible to consult everybody before electing the leader of the community. Some Bedouin (desert dwellers) tribes outside Madinah decided not to accept 'Abu Bakr ﷺ as *Khalifah* of the 'Ummah. Most of these people had just recently become Muslim and had not yet been taught Islamic laws of peaceful coexistence.

The Way of the Bedouin

The Bedouins have been living a rough yet simple lifestyle for thousands of years.

The Bedouin family moves from place to place in order to find grazing land for their flocks of sheep or herds of camels. It is very unusual for a Bedouin tribe to settle in one place permanently. This nomadic way of life caused the Bedouin to be viewed as uncivilized.

The Bedouins have managed to preserve the noble aspects of Arab culture, such as the purity of the Arabic language and their good manners towards their guests and their chivalry in battle.

In fact, most of these tribes revolted against the Islamic state to achieve their personal ambitions. They thought that if the Prophet ﷺ could establish a community and become a leader of the Arabs, they could also do the same. What these tribal leaders did not realize was that Muhammad ﷺ was the last and the final Prophet and Messenger sent and supported by Allah, while they themselves were only pretenders. An important task of 'Abu Bakr ؓ was to eliminate these false prophets and establish the authority of Islam. Some of these tribes mobilized themselves and launched attacks on Madinah itself.

Some of them now declared that they

Rasulullah ﷺ. These moves violated the teachings of the Qur'an.

Although a large number of Muslims had gone to fight in Syria under the leadership of 'Usamah ibn Zaid ؓ, 'Abu Bakr ؓ managed to repel the attack on Madinah from the Bedouin tribes. Then he turned the army toward the false prophets and those tribes who had declared that they would defy the Qur'anic injunction on

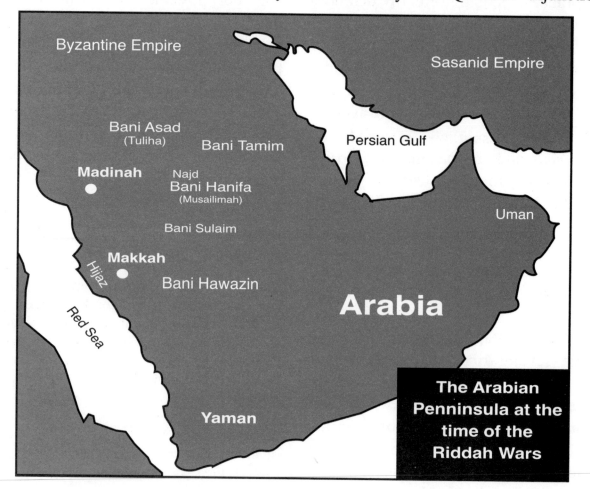

The Arabian Penninsula at the time of the Riddah Wars

would not pay the poor-tax and would not share their wealth with the poor living in various parts of the Muslim world. Others even claimed that they had a new prophet for their own tribe and, therefore, they would not follow the teachings of

Zakah. A number of individuals, including one woman, declared themselves as prophets. Among them were Tulaiha of the Bani 'Asad tribe and Musailimah of the Bani Hanifah tribe of Najd. An ambitious young lady Sajah de-clared herself a prophetess. Later she got married to Musailimah and accepted him as her leader.

Musailimah was the most notorious among all these false prophets. He once visited Madinah during the *lifetime* of Rasulullah ﷺ. After talking to him, Rasulullah ﷺ told his *Sahabah* that Musailimah was a liar. After that, he was known as Musailimah *Al Kadhdhab,* the Liar. After the death of Rasulullah ﷺ, Musailimah declared that he was a prophet and that everybody should follow him. But *Khalifah* 'Abu Bakr ﷺ knew that he was lying, therefore, did not want him to deceive and mislead the people. 'Abu Bakr ﷺ declared war on him. He dispatched the famous general Khalid ibn Al Walid ﷺ who achieved decisive victory over the army of Musailimah the Liar.

Similarly, other revolts also were suppressed. Arabia again became calm and disciplined under the leadership of 'Abu Bakr ﷺ. These wars against false prophets and apostates are known as *Riddah* wars in history. These wars took place during the 11th and 12th year of *Hijrah* or 632 to 633 C.E.

Words and Terms to Remember:

1. *Apostate:*
   One who returns to *Kufr* (disbelief) after accepting Islam.

2. *Jahiliyyah:*
   Ignorance; refers to the period in Arabia before Islam.

3. *Bedouin:*
   Arab tribes which roam in the desert.

4. *Pretender:*
   One who pretends to be something, but when in fact, he is not.

5. *Riddah :*
   Apostasy, a Muslim's leaving the religion of Islam.

6. *Zakah:*
   The amount of wealth to be paid to the poor on one's savings.

We Have Learned:

- After assuming power, 'Abu Bakr ﷺ had to fight against many Arab tribes who revolted against Islam and the state of Madinah.

- After the death of Rasulullah ﷺ, some Arabian tribes declined to pay *Zakah* and 'Abu Bakr ﷺ decided to fight them.

- The false prophets were one by one defeated in the *Riddah* wars by the Islamic forces.

The Spread of Islam: Iraq and Syria

'Abu Bakr ﷺ faced another problem from the two big powers of the time. The Empires of Byzantines (The Eastern Roman) and the Sasanids (The Persians) were fighting each other for the control of the territories in Syria, Palestine, Iraq, Egypt, and Anatolia. They fought a number of battles during the lifetime of the Prophet ﷺ. These two mighty empires did not like the rise of a new force on the political horizon of Arabia which was gradually challenging their oppressive authority in the regions they ruled. Therefore, 'Abu Bakr ﷺ had to devote his time and energy for the defense of the Muslim 'Ummah against these two empires.

The campaigns against the false prophets succeeded not only in crushing their power, but also in attracting many new tribes to Islam. Some of these tribes lived on the border between Arabia and the mighty Sasanid Persian and Byzantine empires. Others lived inside these two empires. Neither of these empires looked with favor to the rise of the new Islamic power in Arabia.

The Arabs, after accepting Islam, experienced the Truth and were now convinced that the Islamic way of life was the best; they showed great enthusiasm to spread the Message to other lands. They had already been visiting areas outside Arabia in connection with their business. Now, along with their business, they also started to propagate Islam.

Rasulullah ﷺ himself had written letters to both the Byzantine and Sasanid emperors inviting them to accept Islam. It is reported that the Byzantine emperor, Heraclius responded positively to the letter and expresssed his intention to become a Muslim. But members of his court prevented him from doing so. They said, "We are Christians and if you want to be our ruler, you must remain a Christian. Otherwise, you will lose your power." The emperor thus failed to openly accept Islam. The Sasanid emperor, Khosrau, on the other hand, abused the ambassador sent by Rasulullah ﷺ and embarked on hostile relations with Muslims.

Iraq, at that time, was under the rule of the Sasanid emperor. During the *Riddah* Wars, the Persians assisted the enemies of Islam. They continued harassing Muslims within their territories even after the end of the war. 'Al-Muthanna ibn Harithah, a Muslim leader, was the chief of the Bani Bakr tribe who lived on the Eastern border between Arabia and Iraq. 'Al-Muthanna continued to help the Muslims who lived under Sasanid Persian rule. But soon he realized his limits and went to Madinah to ask the *Khalifah* for assistance against the Sasanids. After listening carefully to Al-Muthanna, 'Abu Bakr ﷺ decided to send Khalid ibn Al-Walid, the famous Muslim commander, to assist Muthanna and other Muslims who were under pressure from the Sasanid Persians.

Khalid ibn Al-Walid ﷺ proceeded with his army to assist Al-Muthanna against the Sasanids. The Sasanids greatly outnumbered the Muslims. There were several fierce confrontations between the two armies. Finally, Muslims achieved victory over the Sasanids after a long struggle. It was, in fact the faith and enthusiasm of the Muslims which secured them a great victory against a superior enemy. Muslims offered special prayers thanking Allah ﷻ for their victory.

'Usamah ibn Zaid ﷺ led an expedition to Syria in order to punish the tribes that had killed one of the messengers of Rasulullah ﷺ. After 'Usamah's ﷺ successful march, *Khalifah* 'Abu Bakr ﷺ nominated Khalid ibn Al-Walid ﷺ to organize the Muslims who lived in the Syrian region. Like Muthanna in Iraq, Khalid ibn Al-Walid also faced similar problems in dealing with the large size of the Byzantine army. Syria at that time, as we already know, was under the rule of the Byzantine empire.

Khalid ibn Al-Walid ﷺ requested help from Madinah. 'Abu Bakr ﷺ dispatched an army to Syria under the leadership of 'Abu Ubaidah and 'Amr ibn al-'As ﷺ. Under the new leadership, Muslims received initial victory, but they got into some new troubles when the Byzantine reorganized their forces. They also outnumbered the Muslims. When the Muslim position became critical, 'Abu Ubaidah ﷺ sent an emergency message to the *Khalifah* for more Muslim reinforcements. Madinah was almost empty of young men. Those who were able to fight had already gone either to Iraq or to Syria. *Khalifah* 'Abu Bakr ﷺ instructed Khalid ibn Al-Walid ﷺ, who was fighting the Persians in Iraq, to join the Muslim forces in Syria. The regular route to Syria from Iraq required a time-consuming journey. But Khalid ﷺ adopted a new route which was shorter but more dangerous. The danger lay in the fact that there was no water on the way. So Khalid ﷺ invented a new method to face the situation. He collected a number of good camels which could run as fast as the horses, loaded them with plenty of water, and then set out for Syria. Whenever he needed water, he used to slaughter a camel, drink the water loaded on it, eat its meat and proceed further. Thus, he arrived in Syria in less than half the time needed to travel the regular route. This unique method of marching used by Khalid ibn Al-Walid ﷺ is still remembered by historians and military generals.

Immediately, after their arrival in Syria, Khalid ibn Al-Walid ﷺ and his forces encountered the large Byzantine army. By the Grace of Allah, the Muslims won. Then Khalid ؓ advanced to Damascus, the principal city in Syria. The city was already well protected and after initial defeats, the Byzantines reinforced their position. There-fore, Khalid decided to withdraw and regroup the Muslim army to counter the Byzantine threat.

While the Muslim forces were withdrawing, a group of Muslim women, who had accompanied the army, fell behind. The Byzantines planned to take advantage of this situation. As soon as the Muslim women realized this, they prepared themselves for battle. But how could they fight? They were there only to assist the Muslim army; they themselves had no means to fight. They did not possess weapons. However, Khawlah, the sister of the Muslim general Zarrar, suggested that

they dismantle their tents and use the poles and sticks as weapons. She was able to encourage and prepare all the Muslim women to fight. The Byzantine army, as it advanced, was really surprised to see the courage and strength of the Muslim women. Since then, Khawlah has been known as the "Veiled Knight." Meanwhile, when Khalid ؓ came to know of this situation, he immediately returned and rescued the women. Encouraged by the bold step taken by Muslim women, Khalid ؓ surrounded the city of Damascus to compel the Byzantines to surrender. This siege continued for several months until the Muslims achieved a total victory over the Byzantine Empire in Syria. This happened after the death of the first *Khalifah* 'Abu Bakr ؓ in the 13th year of *Hijrah* or 634 C.E.

We Have Learned:

- The Byzantine emperor Heraclius was willing to accept Islam, but his courtiers refused.

- Khalid ibn Al-Walid ﷺ arrived in Iraq to assist the Muslim army.

- During the *Khilafah* of 'Abu Bakr ﷺ, Syria and Iraq were freed.

Highlights of the Khilafah of Abu Bakr ؓ

'Abu Bakr ؓ was busy suppressing revolts against Islam and strengthening the newly established Islamic state of Madinah. He had very little time left to devote to the progress and welfare of the people. Yet he set a number of examples for Muslim rulers and officials. Before becoming *Khalifah,* he was a moderately rich businessman. But his life style was very simple. He did not have a big house and other comforts of life; he lived like an ordinary person in society.

After becoming *Khalifah,* he continued to work to meet the expenses of his household. Others soon realized that the time of the *Khalifah* is very precious and must not be spent in earning a livelihood, they suggested to pay a salary for the *Khalifah* from the *Bait al-Mal*, the treasury of the government. 'Abu Bakr ؓ was reluctant to accept anything from the people's money. He thought that the wealth of *Bait al-Mal* belonged to the people, and that the ruler had no right to it. But how could he survive and serve the community as their leader? When 'Umar ؓ and other *Sahabah* insisted, he accepted the lowest possible salary from the *Bait al-Mal*. In doing so, he had to minimize the expenses of his household and lower his standard of living.

On the other hand he arranged generous stipends for members of the Prophet's ﷺ family and other *Sahabah* from the *Bait al-Mal*. What a great example was this combination of self-sacrifice and generosity!

Another example that was set by 'Abu Bakr ؓ was his use of *shura* or consultation in running the affairs of the government. The Qur'an taught Muslims that "they consult among themselves in their affairs." (42:38) This teaching of the Qur'an was further elaborated by Rasulullah ﷺ on various occasions. He himself set an example of *shura* in running the affairs of the state. Rasulullah ﷺ was a Prophet guided by *Wahi,* or Revelation, and himself was an authority. He, however, did not need to follow the opinion of the people on every matter. People were advised by Allah ﷻ to follow the Messenger. 'Abu Bakr ؓ was 'Amir Al-Mu'minin, the leader of the Believers, and did not have the same status as the Prophet Muhammad ﷺ. Therefore, his method of consultation became a good lesson to be learned by the later rulers, who needed the opinions of the wisest and most experienced

22

of the Muslims in making their decisions.

Another major contribution of 'Abu Bakr ﷺ was the compilation of the Qur'an into a book form. The Qur'an was revealed in parts over a period of twenty-three years. Whenever a verse or some verses were revealed, the writers would write them accord-ing to the instruction of Rasulullah ﷺ. They used to write on goat or camel skins, or on leaves, or on stones. There was no paper in Arabia in those days. However, many Muslims used to memorize them right away.

In the battles that Muslims had to fight against the false prophets and the Persian and the Byzantine emperors, many Muslims who had memorized the whole Qur'an died. Due to this situation, the leading Muslims became concerned and suggested to 'Abu Bakr ﷺ the compilation of the whole Qur'an in written form and its official preservation. Rasulullah ﷺ had a number of scribes who used to write for him officially. Zaid ibn Thabit ﷺ was a leading scribe of Rasulullah ﷺ. 'Abu Bakr ﷺ assigned Zaid ibn Thabit ﷺ to compile the Qur'an into a book form. When it was done, 'Abu Bakr ﷺ preserved this officially for the benefit of later Muslims.

'Abu Bakr ﷺ also set a good example in the method of nominating his successor. 'Abu Bakr ﷺ fell ill after two years in office. He consulted with leading *Sahabah* of Rasulullah ﷺ about his succession. People generally agreed that 'Umar ibn Al-Khattab should succeed him. On the basis of their opinion, 'Abu Bakr ﷺ declared the official decision by saying,

> "After consulting with most of you, I am nominating 'Umar ﷺ to succeed me as your leader. In the past, he has acted with justice and equity. If he acts with equity and justice and undertakes measures for the welfare of the people, my nomination of him will be proved to be right. If he indulges in injustice and oppression, I will be innocent because I do not know the unseen and base my decision on his past. Allah knows that I mean well."

After a little over two years in office, 'Abu Bakr ﷺ passed away in the 13th year of *Hijrah* or 634 C.E.

Words and Terms to Remember:

1. *Bait al-Mal:*
   Literally "the House of Wealth." It is the government treasury in the Islamic State.

2. *Shura:*
   Consultation or discussion. All affairs of Muslims, the Qur'an advised, must be decided through *shura*.

3. *Nominating:*
   When someone is recommended or chosen for a position or job.

We Have Learned:

- According to 'Abu Bakr ﷺ the wealth of the *Bait al-Mal* belonged to the people.

- 'Abu Bakr ﷺ practiced *shura,* the consultation, in running the affairs of the 'Ummah.

- The Qur'an was originally compiled into a book form by Zaid ibn Thabit ﷺ during the *Khilafah* of 'Abu Bakr ﷺ

'Umar's ؓ inheritance of the Khilafah

After the death of 'Abu Bakr ؓ, 'Umar ibn Al-Khattab ؓ became the leader of the 'Ummah. In the beginning, there was uncertainty about his official title. He succeeded 'Abu Bakr ؓ whose official title was *Khalifatu Rasulullah*. 'Umar ؓ was first called *Khalifatu Khalifati-Rasulullah*, meaning successor to the successor of Rasulullah. But repetition of the word *Khalifah* would prove cumbersome to use in daily speech. Therefore, Muslims introduced a new term for the office *'Amir ul-Mu'minin* or "The leader of the Believers." This sounded attractive to many Muslims. 'Umar ؓ accepted this as the official title of the leader of the 'Ummah.

When the *bai'ah* or declaration of allegiance by the people was over, 'Umar ؓ addressed the Muslims by saying,

"My dear fellow Muslims! 'Abu Bakr is no more with us. He has successfully run the affairs of the 'Ummah for more than two years and successfully performed some of the incomplete tasks of the Prophet ﷺ. I wish the responsibility of leading the 'Ummah had fallen on someone else. I never desired such a position. However, I assure you that I shall not run away from this responsibility. I shall discharge my duty to the best of my ability. I shall seek guidance from the Qur'an, teachings of Rasulullah ﷺ and examples set by 'Abu Bakr ؓ in running the affairs of the government. In this task, I will also seek your participation and assistance. If I am right, follow me. If I deviate, correct me so that we do not go astray. "

Then, 'Umar ؓ prayed to Allah ﷻ saying,

"O Allah, I am told by people that I am hard and strict, please make me soft and lenient to promote the Truth and help me to achieve peace and prosperity in this life and in the Hereafter.

O Allah, make me hard on the enemies of Islam and enemies of humanity so that I can crush those who oppress others and spread mischief in the society.

O Allah, save me from hypocrisy. Help me in doing the things that I say.

O Allah, soften my heart for the Believers so that I can be helpful to them.

O Allah, grant me the understanding of what is good and what is bad so that we can cultivate good and abstain from what is evil.

O Allah, if I am careless, make me responsible so that I can feel for the problems of others as mine.

O Allah, grant me the power of self criticism so that I can understand my mistakes and correct them.

O Allah, grant me the power to fulfill my

responsibilities. *Amin.*"

'Umar again addressed the gathering of Muslims saying,

"Dear fellow Muslims! Many of you say that I was harsh when the Prophet was alive, and I was uncompromising during the rule of 'Abu Bakr. Yes, whenever they consulted with me, I expressed my opinion. Sometimes, they accepted my opinion and sometimes they rejected it. But, thanks to Allah, Rasulullah was pleased with me and so was 'Abu Bakr. Both of them approved my conduct. Now that the responsibility has fallen on me, I shall try to be soft and tender. However, I shall be harsh and strict against an aggressor in favor of the weak and poor. In running the government, you will be my partner. Please help me with your service and advice. If I deviate, stop me. Let us all pray for the glory of Islam."

Words and Terms to Remember:

1. *'Amir Al-Mu'minin:*
   "The Leader of the Believers." This official title of the leader of the *'Ummah,* was adopted during the time of 'Umar.

2. *Responsibility:*
   A duty or a trust given to a person.

3. *Self-criticism:*
   Someone criticizing himself. One's capability to see his own faults and readiness to correct them.

We Have Learned:

- 'Umar adopted the title *'Amir ul-Mu'minin* after he became the *Khalifah.*

- 'Abu Bakr nominated 'Umar for the office of *Khalifah.*

- 'Umar sought Allah's Blessings and people's cooperation in running the affairs of his government.

26

The Early Life of Umar

'Umar ibn Al-Khattab was born in a clan of the Quraish of Makkah in the year 580 C.E. This was about ten years after the birth of Rasulullah. He was one of the few Makkans who could read and write. He was also a famous sportsman; he earned reputation as a wrestler. Professionally, he was a trader and, like Rasulullah and 'Abu Bakr, he had travelled outside 'Arabia in connection with his business. Because of his exceptional qualities and bravery, 'Umar enjoyed enormous

Pre-Islamic Makkan Society

The people of Makkah before the days of Islam were divided into several different social classes. The most powerful people were the leaders of the richest clans and could be assured the benefits of a good life. These clans possessed both wealth and prestige.

After these clans came those clans who weren't as wealthy. Because of their lack of influence they usually had to ally themselves with other more influential clans.

On the bottom of the social ladder were those who did not belong to any of the influential clans and those who were slaves. Their condi-

power and influence in Arabia. During the early days of the Prophethood when only

few individuals accepted Islam, Rasulullah specially prayed for 'Umar ibn Al-Khattab to become a Muslim. The Blessed Prophet thought that his inclusion among the Muslims would strengthen them significantly.

'Umar's acceptance of Islam is an interesting story. 'Umar used to have very short temper before he accepted Islam. Once he learned that one of his maidservants had accepted Islam. He was a bitter enemy of Islam at that time. He called the servant, inquired about her new belief he came very angry with her. After a while, when 'Umar asked her whether she would leave Islam, she boldly answered, "No." The proud 'Umar could not tolerate such a bold refusal. He came very upset and started to beat her. It was in vain. Tired and angry, 'Umar then decided to eradicate Islam at its root. He decided to kill Rasulullah. As he left home with his sword, he met a friend who had become a Muslim but did not disclose his conversion because of fear of the Quraish.

"Where are you heading, O 'Umar?" asked his friend Nu'aim ibn 'Abdullah.

"I am fed up with Muhammad and I am

going to kill him," said 'Umar.

Nu'aim ﷺ immediately responded saying, "Do you know what will happen if you kill him? The entire family of Bani Hashim will retaliate against you. Even though many of them are not Muslims, they have a great respect for Muhammad."

"It seems you also have become a Muslim," remarked 'Umar angrily.

"Forget about me," Nu'aim ﷺ replied. "Do you know that your sister Fatimah and her husband Sa'id have accepted Islam? Take care of your family first!"

All of a sudden, 'Umar changed his course. Instead of going to Rasulullah ﷺ, he headed toward his sister's home. Nu'aim ﷺ, of course, ran straight to warn Rasulullah ﷺ.

'Umar loved his sister very much. But his anger and hatred against Islam made him lose his senses. His sister Fatimah ﷺ and her husband, Sa'id ﷺ, were reading the Qur'an written on a leaf when the angry 'Umar reached their home. Fatimah ﷺ immediately hid the leaf, as soon as she noticed 'Umar entering her home, but 'Umar had already seen it. When he questioned them, both Fatimah ﷺ and Sa'id ﷺ admitted that they had accepted Islam and had not disclosed it for fear of the Quraish. The angry 'Umar would not tolerate this. He started to beat Sa'id ﷺ. Fatimah ﷺ came to resist 'Umar and he slapped her in the face.

When 'Umar saw Fatimah's ﷺ bruised cheek, he stopped. He loved his sister so much that he could not bear this scene. He understood that he was behaving in a senseless manner. When he calmed down, 'Umar asked Sa'id ﷺ and Fatimah ﷺ to show him what they were reading before he had arrived. 'Umar wanted to hold the written leaf in his hand. But Fatimah ﷺ told him he could not touch it as he was unclean.

So 'Umar washed himself. He then took the leaf of the Qur'an to see what his sister and brother-in-law were reading. It was part of *Surah Ta-Ha*. He read the verses again and again. As he read them, he became convinced that those verses could not be written by a human being. As a learned man, he realized that a man like Muhammad ﷺ, who never had any formal education, could not possibly write a fine piece of literature like that. Umar's heart was deeply touched.

"I am convinced that Muhammad is the real Prophet and Messenger of God," said 'Umar, "and I want to become a Muslim."

Tears of joy flowed from the eyes of Fatimah ﷺ and Sa'id ﷺ. It was a happy moment for them.

From there, 'Umar ﷺ went directly to the house of Rasulullah's ﷺ. He still had the sword with him. When Muslims saw 'Umar coming to see Rasulullah ﷺ with a drawn sword they became alert. They hesitated to allow him to enter the house.

When Rasulullah ﷺ himself noticed this, he asked the followers to let him enter the house. 'Umar entered and declared, "O Rasulullah ﷺ, I have made mistakes. Now I realize my mistakes, and I want to accept Islam."

Everybody, including Rasulullah ﷺ himself, was overjoyed and there were shouts of *"Allah-u 'Akbar!"* Allah ﷻ answered Rasulullah's ﷺ prayers regarding 'Umar ﷺ. Now that 'Umar had become a Muslim, he led Rasulullah ﷺ and his followers to the *Ka'bah* to offer prayer in public.

The days of preaching Islam *(da'wah)* in secret were now over, and with 'Umar's ﷺ acceptance of Islam a new phase began in the history of Islam. After that, 'Umar ﷺ was closely associated with all major events of Islam under Rasulullah ﷺ himself and under the first *Khalifah* 'Abu Bakr ﷺ.

Words and Terms to Remember:

1. *Bani Hashim:*
   The Family of Hashim. Hashim was the great-grandfather of Rasulullah ﷺ. His family was very influential in Makkah.

2. *Da'wah:*
   Preaching and inviting others to the message of Islam.

We Have Learned:

- 'Umar ﷺ was an influential person in Makkah.

- 'Umar ﷺ was a bitter enemy of Islam before he became a Muslim.

- After listening to the Qur'an, 'Umar's ﷺ heart softened toward the Muslims and he accepted Islam.

The Spread of Islam in Iraq

The *Khilafah* of 'Umar ﷺ contributed to great expansion of Islam in all directions. The powerful empires of Persia and Byzantine first resisted Islamic power and tried to nip it in the bud. Still, Muslims scored one victory after another over their enemies. Soon the two empires started crumbling before the advance of Muslim armies. We shall here discuss the spread of Islam in Iraq, then part of the Persian Empire.

Many Arab tribes on the borders between Arabia, Syria, and Iraq had accepted Islam. Syria at that time was under the Eastern Roman Empire. This great empire is more commonly known as the Byzantine Empire. Iraq, on the other hand, was a part of the mighty Sasanid Persian Empire. Both empires shared a long border and they fought many bloody wars against each other for nearly four hundred years. The Qur'an mentions

their last great war in *Surah 'Ar-Rum* (The Romans).

Neither of those two empires liked the rise of Islam. Both of them were expansionists and wanted to control as much land as possible. After conquering areas by force, they imposed heavy taxes on the local people. With this tax money, the leaders of these

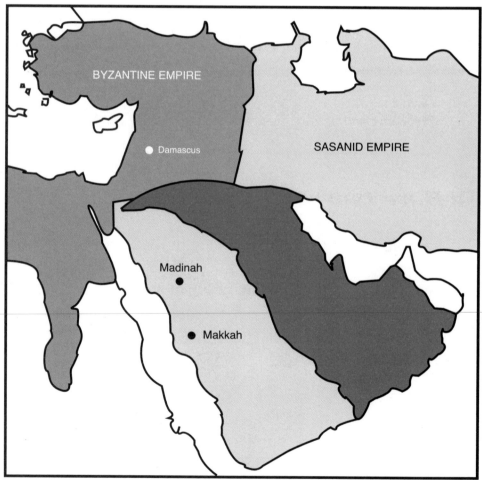

30

empires used to enjoy lives in extreme luxury. They would not care for the wellbeing of their citizens. That is why the people of Syria were not happy with the Byzantine rulers, nor the Iraqis with their Sasanid rulers.

When the Muslim Arab tribes of Syria needed military assistance, the first *Khalifah,* 'Abu Bakr ﷺ, instructed Khalid ibn Al-Walid ﷺ to move there immediately from Iraq. This caused the local tribal chief, Muthanna ﷺ, to be left alone to face the might of the Sasanid army. Although the Sasanids had become very weak after years of fighting against the Byzantines and they had just recently lost to the Muslims, they were able to reorganize and regroup their forces. Therefore, Muthanna ﷺ personally went to Madinah to request *Khalifah* 'Abu Bakr ﷺ for more troops to help them against the Sasanid Persians again.

The Islamic State of Madinah did not have a permanent army in those days. There were no professional salaried armed men to defend and protect their lands, government or people. Every Muslim was expected to be a defender of the Islamic State. Therefore, Muthanna ﷺ appealed to the Muslims of Madinah directly to go to help defend Islam in Iraq.

'Umar ibn Al-Khattab ﷺ succeeded 'Abu Bakr ﷺ during Muthanna's ﷺ stay in Madinah. As soon as he became *Khalifah* his first task was to appeal to people to rise and fight the enemy. The Muslims were

able to organize an army which was placed under the leadership of 'Abu 'Ubaidah ibn 'Al-Jarrah ﷺ and they marched to Iraq to fight the Sasanid Persians.

In the meantime, the Sasanids prepared a great army to face the Muslims. After a brief struggle over who would lead the Empire, a young prince named Yazdigerd was made *Shahinshah,* the Emperor of all

The Warriors of Islam

The early Muslim soldiers were often outnumbered by the armies of their more powerful enemies and the quality of their weapons and armor were often no match to their enemies.

Those Muslims who could afford to do so, often equipped themselves with weapons and armor of better quality, but the average Muslim soldier went on foot without any armor except for a rough leather shield for protection.

When marching against the enemy, the Muslim army would use the desert to outflank the opposing army. The Byzantines and Sasanids had a justifiable fear about marching any of their forces into the Arabian desert.

In battle, a portion of the army would fight on foot and another would do so mounted on either horses or camels. During the early days, horses were scarcely found in Muslim ranks. But as more of the rich lands of the Middle East were conquered, the Muslim army came into the possesion of more and more horses.

However, the most important factor in the Muslim armies was not the number of men or the superiority of weaponry, but a firm belief in Allah and a lack of fear of death in battle, something which the average Byzantine or Persian soldier lacked.

Persia. But the real leadership was in the hands of a general by the name of Rustam. This commander organized a huge force numbering more than one hundred thousand soldiers. This army was made up of many different kinds of soldiers. There were men clad in armor from head to foot, carrying long lances and mounted on war horses. There were light horsemen skilled in archery and there were huge elephants, on the backs of which were tied small forts full of men with bows and spears.

But there were also large numbers of peasants who were forced into the army by their Sasanid lords. They marched into battle with little more than a straw shield and a spear. They had always been badly treated and they had very little commitment to fight for an emperor who exploited them. The Sasanids also imposed high taxes on the people in Iraq to pay for their huge army. Therefore, the local Iraqis, like most of the people of Persia, did not put all their effort in fighting the Muslims. In fact, they favored the Muslims against the Sasanids.

When Muthanna ﷺ and 'Abu 'Ubaidah ﷺ returned to Iraq to help the Muslims, the Muslims were ill equipped. They had only a few hundred soldiers and their weapons and armors were no match for the well-armed Sasanid soldiers. The Muslims could not hold the attack of the Sasanid army and they were defeated. Both 'Abu 'Ubaidah and Muthanna ﷺ became *Shuhada'* (martyrs) in the battle. A *shahid* goes straight to Paradise, according to Muslim beliefs.

This alarmed the *Khalifah* in Madinah. He again appealed to the Muslims in Madinah to go to help their brothers in Iraq. This

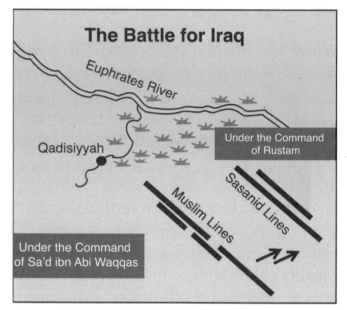

The Battle for Iraq

Euphrates River

Qadisiyyah

Under the Command of Rustam

Sasanid Lines

Muslim Lines

Under the Command of Sa'd ibn Abi Waqqas

time, more than four thousand Muslims un-der the leadership of Sa'd ibn 'Abi Waqqas ﷺ left Madinah to face the Sasanid forces in Iraq. One of the false prophets, Tulaihah (who had now embraced Islam) also joined the Muslims.

The Muslim army went to Iraq and camped near a village called Qadisiyyah. Here, several thousand Muslim soldiers encountered an army of more than 120,000 well-armed Sasanid troops. The Muslims fought courageously with great skill. They had strong faith and devotion. They also received assistance from the local population who supported the Muslims because of the Sasanids oppression.

In the battle, Muslims won a stunning victory. The Sasanid Commander-in-Chief,

Rustam, was killed in the battle and gradually the whole of Iraq came under the control of the Muslims. This was in the 14th year of *Hijrah* or 636 C.E. This opened the way for the Muslims to spread the message of Islam in Persia itself.

Most of the people of Iraq and Persia at that time were either Zoroastrians or Christians.

The Muslims did not force the Iraqis or the Persians to change their religion. By their good behavior and fair treatment of the people, Muslims convinced the local populations of the beauty of Islam. Over the centuries, most Iraqis and Persians came to accept Islam as their *Din*.

Words and Terms to Remember:

1. *Expansionist:*
   A desire to take control of other countries.

2. *Ill-equipped:*
   To have little or no equipment.

3. *Shahinshah:*
   The "King of Kings." The title of the Sasanid emperor.

4. *Shahid:*
   Someone who is killed in the Way of Islam, also a witness.

We Have Learned:

- The Byzantine and Sasanid rulers oppressed the people of Syria and Iraq.

- The Muslims defeated the Persian army at the battle of Qadisiyyah.

- Most people of Iraq and Persia accepted Islam.

Syria Comes Under Muslim Control

The rise of Islam in the world was challeng-ed not only by the Sasanid Persian Empire, but also by the Byzantine Empire. Rasulullah ﷺ wrote a letter to the Byzantine emperor inviting him to accept Islam. According to some historians, the emperor wanted to accept Islam, but his officials prevented him from doing so. The officials told him that if he became a Muslim he would lose his empire, because most people under his rule were Christians. The emperor, whose name was Heraclius, therefore, did not become a muslim. But gradually, people under his rule became Muslims and the emperor lost control over one country after the other. All this began with Syria.

During the *Khilafah* of 'Abu Bakr ﷺ, Muslims went to punish one of the small rulers on the border between Arabia and Syria because the ruler had killed the ambassador of Rasulullah ﷺ. After that, local Muslims came under attack by the Byzantine army. The Muslims from Madinah went to assist them and they succeeded in defeating the Byzantines. Under the leadership of Khalid ibn Al-Walid ﷺ, they besieged the city of Damascus.

Big cities in those days used to be sur-

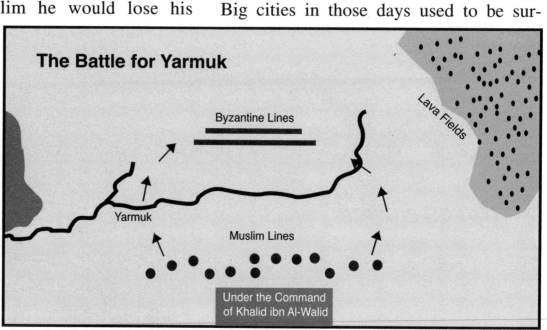

The Battle for Yarmuk

Byzantine Lines

Lava Fields

Yarmuk

Muslim Lines

Under the Command of Khalid ibn Al-Walid

rounded by large and thick walls that offered excellent defense. Damascus had high walls with a number of gates. Therefore, the entrance routes to the city were limited. Even now you may find walls around some of those ancient cities. Khalid ibn Al-Walid ﷺ did not want to shed blood unnecessarily. Therefore, he camped outside the city and stopped supplies entering the city. But the Byzantine rulers of the city decided not to surrender. This meant a continuation of suffering of the local population.

The Muslims continued the siege of Damascus for more than six months. Finally, Khalid ibn Al-Walid 🕮 decided to storm the city. He recruited some brave volunteers to climb over the high walls in order to enter the city and open the gates for the Muslim army. As soon as the Muslim army entered the city, the Byzantine rulers of the city surrendered, and the city was finally captured on 14 Hijrah or 636 C.E. The loss of Damascus alarmed the Byzantines. As a big power, the Byzantine Empire had not considered the rise of Islam a serious threat to their power in Syria. But after the loss of Damascus, the Byzantine emperor, Heraclius, called his troops from various parts of his empire to turn the Muslims back. The two armies met each other at a place called Yarmuk in the year 15 *Hijrah* or 637 C.E. The number of Byzantine forces according to some estimates was almost a quarter of a million, while there were only about forty thousand Muslims to face them.

The Muslims won a decisive victory. This was possible due to the Muslims faith, theircourage, and the assistance of the local population. After this battle, the Byzantine army was gradually forced out of Syria.

Words and Terms to Remember:

1. *Besiege:*
   To surround a city and try to capture it using various methods.

2. *Byzantium:*
   Original name of Istanbul, also Constantinople, seat of Byzantine Empire.

3. *Byzantine Empire:*
   Eastern Roman Empire which ruled from Constantinople.

We Have Learned:

- All big cities in the time of the *Khulafa'* were protected by big, thick walls.

- Khalid ibn Al-Walid 🕮 led the Muslim forces which captured Damascus after a siege of six months.

- Gradually, the Byzantine army was forced out of Syria.

Palestine and Egypt are Liberate

In those days, Byzantium also ruled over Palestine and Egypt. Palestine was a part of the province of Syria, while Egypt was a separate province. Jerusalem *(Bait ul-Maqdis or 'Al-Quds)* was located in Palestine and it was a center of Christianity. The Jews had very close spiritual ties to Palestine also and regarded it as their "promised land." The Christian rulers of Jerusalem, however, did not accept their claim and did not even allow them to enter into that Christian city.

The Muslims also had spiritual links to Jerusalem. Before the *Hijrah* to Madinah, and during the early days in Madinah, Muslims used to pray toward Jerusalem. Many blessed prophets of Allah had lived in that land and were buried in or near Jerusalem. Rasulullah ﷺ in the night of *Isra'* and *Mi'raj* (Ascension) was first taken to Jerusalem where he met all the prophets in the *'Al-Masjid Al-'Aqsa*. He led them in prayer and then he ascended to Heaven.

When most of Syria was conquered by the Muslims, the Byzantine forces left Jerusalem. The Christian religious leaders of Jerusalem immediately informed the leaders of the Muslim army that the people

Christianity in the Byzantine World

Six centuries before Rasulullah ﷺ, after the Messenger 'Isa ﷺ had left the world, his message became corrupted and changed. His followers spread throughout the Mediterranean world preaching Christianity, professing many forms of doctrines.

The pagan Roman religion believed in many gods and goddesses. They imposed their religion on all of their subjects. At first, Christians were persecuted for their beliefs about God by the pagan Roman government. But in the fourth century, Roman emperor Constantine had a vision in which 'Isa ﷺ asked him to abandon paganism and become a Christian. From that moment on, the Roman (and later Byzantine) Empire became officially Christian.

Many people within the Christian religion had different views about the nature of God and His prophet, 'Isa ﷺ. Some said that God was One and that 'Isa ﷺ was only a human messenger. Others said no, that God was a Trinity made up of Himself, 'Isa ﷺ, as the Son, and the Holy Spirit. They also said that 'Isa ﷺ was, in fact, God incarnated in human flesh! These Christians were further divided into groups who argued over whether 'Isa ﷺ was the physical son of God or only His spiritual son or if 'Isa ﷺ was both God and human or completely God!

In 325 C.E., the Roman (Byzantine) emperor proclaimed that the doctrine of the Trinity was to be the only true belief about God. Other Christians were subjected to persecution and harrassment by the official Church.

of Jerusalem would like to submit to the *Khalifah*, if he himself would travel to Jerusalem and guarantee their religious freedom. Therefore, the desire of the leaders of Jerusalem for the *Khalifah* 'Umar to personally accept the surrender of the city was communicated to him in Madinah. It was not easy to travel from Madinah to Jerusalem in those days. This was particularly true for 'Umar, because he did not believe in imposing his needs on people. Neither did he believe in bodyguards or royal entourages. Yet, 'Umar did not want to reject the offer of the Christian leaders of Jerusalem and he wanted to avoid bloodshed at any cost. Besides, he believed that his visit could create the goodwill between Christians and Muslims and be an example for future relations.

'Umar left Madinah for Jerusalem on camel with only one attendant. A servant is necessary in a desert journey because while one person rides on the camel the other person is needed to pull the rope of the camel forward in the desired direction. After crossing some distance from the city of Madinah, 'Umar descended from the camel and asked the servant to ride on it in order to share the camel ride equally. This surprised the servant even though he knew 'Umar's concern for equality and justice. In response to his servant 'Umar said,

> "We both are equal in the sight of Allah. That one of us is the *Khalifah* and the other is an attendant is not fate, but an accident of history. I could have been an attendant and you could have been the *Khalifah*.

Because of the fact that you are an attendant, I should not let you pull the camel all the time. Both of us are humans and both of us are crossing the desert; we should share the desert's heat equally. Please don't increase my burden as the *Khalifah* on the Day of Judgment, when Allah will hold me responsible for all my actions. If I don't treat you justly, how can I expect Justice from Allah?"

Thus 'Umar, the *Khalifah* of Islam, set a great example of social equality in history.

When 'Umar reached Jerusalem it was his turn to walk. The leaders of Jerusalem were surprised. They could not believe themselves that the *Khalifah* of the Muslims must be walking on foot and his servant sitting on the camel. Nor could they believe that the ruler of such a great empire could be such a simple person. As they talked to him they discovered how sincere and honest a person he was.

He was very warmly received everywhere he went. Rarely ever before in the history of any city such a peaceful conquest took place. One is reminded of the liberation of Makkah a few years ago. 'Umar was taken around by the Christian priests to the Church of the Holy Sepulcher, one of the most sacred Christian churches. The Christians believe that 'Isa was buried there after his crucification. As 'Umar was going through the Church, the time for *'Asr* prayer approached. 'Umar wanted to get out of the church and offer prayer outside. The church leaders invited him to offer prayer inside the church. He declined the offer saying,

"The Qur'an recognizes the Jews and the Christians as 'Ahl Al-Kitab (People of the Book) and provides them full freedom of religion. If I offer my prayers inside the Church, tomorrow Muslims may usurp it, because of my offering prayers, and turn it into a *masjid*."

There is indeed a *masjid* on the spot outside the Church where 'Umar ؓ prayed that day. Muslims in their long history followed the example of 'Umar ؓ and respected the holy places of other religions. The Church of the Holy Sepulcher is still a very important place of Christian worship. Thus, in the spirit of tolerance and truth, Jerusalem was captured. It must also be noted that 'Umar ؓ must have seen the cross and the statues of Jesus, Mary and other saints in the Church. He did not break any nor did anything to show his disapproval. He knew Islam more than most Muslim scholars of his time, and he understood that Islam is a religion of toler

ance and understanding. He believed that through love and teaching, one day these people will understand Islam and give up false beliefs. This, indeed happened soon and most of the people in Jerusalem, Syria, and Palestine became Muslims through their own accord.

In the land of Egypt further to the West, most Egyptians did not follow the branch of Christianity that was approved of by the Byzantine government. In fact, because of the religious persecution by the Byzantines, the Egyptians also were looking for liberators. The Muslim general, 'Amr ibn Al-'As responded to this desire. When 'Amr came to know about the unhappiness of the Egyptian people, he sought permission from the *Khalifah* 'Umar ibn Al-Khattab to liberate Egypt from Byzantine rule. The *Khalifah* gave him permission to advance into Egypt and the land of the Nile was captured in 20 A.H or 641 C.E.

Church of the Holy Sepulchre Today, a living and important symbol of the tolerance of Islam!

A testimony of 'Umar's ؓ toleration

Words and Terms to Remember:

1. *'Ahl Al-Kitab:* "The People of the Book." This particularly means Jews, Christians and Sabeans who followed books revealed by Allah to earlier prophets.

2. *Bait ul-Maqdis:*
   "The House of Sanctity or Holiness" or *Al-Quds:* The "Sanctified Place" or Holy Place. Islamic names of Jerusalem.

3. *Buraq:*
   The animal that carried Rasulullah ﷺ from Makkah to Jerusalem and then up into the Heavens.

4. *Crucifixion:*
   The Christian belief that 'Isa ﷺ died on the cross for the sins of mankind.

5. *'Al-Masjid 'Al-'Aqsa:*
   The Farthest Mosque, the *Masjid* in Jerusalem originally built by Prophet Dawud ﷺ and his son Sulaiman ﷺ.

6. *'Isra'* and *Mi'raj:*
   Rasulullah's ﷺ night journey from Makkah to Jerusalem and from Jerusalem to heavens. ﷺ and his son Sulaiman ﷺ.

We Have Learned:

- Muslims have special relations with Jews and Christians; the Qur'an calls them *'Ahl Al-Kitab* or "People of the Book."

- Jerusalem was liberated peacefully, and Muslims treated all the citizens generously.

- 'Umar ﷺ prayed outside the Church of the Holy Sepulchre so that Muslims would not convert this place of Christian worship into a mosque.

'Umar ﷺ: An Exemplary Ruler

During the ten years of his *Khilafah,* 'Umar ﷺ made a remarkable contribution in the history of Islam. 'Umar ﷺ was a man with very high moral qualities. He practiced all the good qualities himself before instructing others to do so. Once during his rule there was a famine in Arabia. As the *Khalifah,* he tried to make sure that everybody received a small amount of dates, milk, and bread to survive. He himself did not eat anything other than dates and bread during this period though he could have afforded more. As the *Khalifah,* he believed it was his responsibility to make sure that all the people received food before he himself ate.

During these years, he took a number of ad-ministrative steps which became important for the growth of the *'Ummah.* Under his leadership Islam spread to many lands. He divided the Muslim controlled areas into eight provinces. He appointed pious and capable governors to all these provinces. He instructed the newly appointed governors in the following words:

> "I am not sending you as a tyrant ruler. I am sending you only as a leader so that people can follow you as a good example. You should make sure that everybody enjoys equal and due rights. Don't beat or humiliate anybody and do not praise anybody to make him a victim of self-pride. Make sure that the strong do not overpower the weak in any matter because that will be a great injustice."

Following the example of 'Abu Bakr ﷺ, 'Umar ﷺ himself used to draw the minimum possible salary from the public treasury. He also fixed the salaries of the governors. He believed that the wealth of the gov-ernment treasury belonged to the people, and administrators were only custodians of that money. He did not allow accumulation of money in the public treasury. When the income of the government increased significantly, he made arrangements to distribute the wealth to the common people. He announced an allowance for everybody in Madinah. Those who became Muslims earlier, made the *Hijrah,* and participated in the battles received a larger allowance than those who accepted Islam later.

'Umar ﷺ employed a number of individuals to inform him about problems of the people. He used to go around in the streets of Madinah to find out the conditions of the citizens. Once as he was in his nightly rounds, he suddenly noticed a poor woman in a hut trying to cook something and to pacify a number of small children. When he approached the lady, he came to know that she did not have anything to feed the children. She was pretending to cook something only to show the children that she was cooking for them. She was hoping the children would go to sleep, waiting for the food to be prepared. 'Umar ؓ became very sad when he saw this. He immediately rushed to his home, got some bread, milk, and dates, fed the children and put them to sleep. The poor woman then said,

> "I don't know who you are. But one thing I know for sure that you are a better person than 'Umar. He is our *Khalifah,* but he does not know that I have nothing to eat at home. Tell me, how good is our *Khalifah,* if he does not care for us."

'Umar ؓ nodded in agreement and said,

> "Yes, you are right; 'Umar is responsible for your welfare. Please forgive 'Umar this time, for he has learned his lesson."

'Umar was overwhelmed with emotions. He turned to Allah for help and forgiveness,

> "O Allah, you have entrusted me with a great responsibility. I know that even if a dog dies without food in my territory, I shall be responsible. But I am weak and sometimes I fail to fulfill my duty. Please forgive me and help me. Please strengthen my ability to perform my duty."

The poor woman soon came to know the identity of 'Umar; she was overjoyed and thanked Allah ﷻ for giving the *'Um-mah* such a great *Khalifah.*

Words and Terms to Remember:

1. *Identity:*
   Characteristics which are particular to a person with which he is recognized.

2. *Province:*
   A large administrative district of a country.

3. *Salary :*
   The pay that a person receives for his work.

We Have Learned:

- 'Umar ؓ appointed pious and capable governors in his administration.

- 'Umar ؓ always practiced himself first what he preached before he ordered others to do the same.

- 'Umar ؓ used to walk in the streets of Madinah to find out about the condition of the people under his rule.

Administration of 'Umar ﷺ

'Umar ﷺ was not only a loving and caring *Khalifah,* but he was also a good administrator. He divided the Muslim world into provinces. 'Umar ﷺ made sure that the governors of those provinces were good Muslims and efficient administrators. He was greatly concerned that the people living outside the capital city of Madinah received similar care and justice as did the people of Madinah.

Along with the governors, he appointed *Qudah* (*Qadi* sing.) or judges, for each of the provinces. Earlier, the governors themselves used to work as *Qudah.* But as the governors assumed more responsibilities, they needed people to help them in their duties. There was a separation of powers between administrative and judicial officials. The separation of powers means that both the judiciary and executive be independent of each other, while they must work together.

Like 'Abu Bakr ﷺ, 'Umar ﷺ maintained the institution of *shura,* or consultation, for the running of the affairs of the government. In his consultations, he gave preference to early Muslims who had spent most time with the Prophet ﷺ and sacrificed most for Islam. Anybody could ask any question to the *Khalifah* about the government or private dealings. There were no formalities required to meet the *Khalifah.*

Another important contribution of 'Umar ﷺ was the introduction of the new *Hijrah* calendar. During the pre-Islamic times, the Arabs counted months but not years. They used to calculate years based on major events. For example, they used to identify the year of Rasulullah's ﷺ birth as the "Year of the Elephant." This was when the Christian ruler of Yemen, Abraha, invaded Makkah with an army, among which were many elephants. But he failed to destroy the *Ka'bah.* On the contrary, he himself perished along with his army. The Arabs of Makkah called this year the "Year of the Elephant." Allah ﷻ also confirmed this event in the Qur'an *(Al-Fil: 104).*

During the rule of 'Umar ﷺ, some of his officials suggested to him that identification of days and months was not accurate enough and that they also needed to identify years. This was necessary to know the time when letters were written and official orders were issued. Everybody agreed with the idea of a calendar; but a question arose about when to begin counting the new calendar. Some suggested counting from the birth of Rasulullah ﷺ, while others suggested to begin from the *Hijrah* or the Migration of the Prophet ﷺ from Makkah to Madinah.

This proposal was acceptable to most people. However, the exact time of Migration did not fall on the first day of a month. According to the pre-Islamic Arabs, the year began with the month of *Muharram,* and the Migration had taken place in the month of *Rabi' 'Al-'Awwal.* After discussion, *Muharram* was retained as the first month of the new calendar. Since they started to count from the time of *Hijrah,* the new calendar came to be known as the *Hijrah* calendar.

During the *Khilafah* of 'Umar ﷺ, the conquest of new lands encouraged thousands of people to embrace Islam. This dramatic increase in the number of Muslims also meant the increase in the number of the pilgrims to Makkah. With this in mind, *Khalifah* 'Umar ﷺ embarked on a project to enlarge the sanctuary around the *Ka'bah* to accommodate the large numbers of pilgrims. 'Umar ﷺ took many other steps to improve the condition of common people within the Muslim world. He ensured fair treatment of all, regardless of wealth, influence, or reli-gious affiliation. He constructed a number of canals in Egypt and Syria to increase agricultural production in those areas. He also made sure that Muslims from Makkah and Madinah did not acquire private property in these newly conquered provinces without using proper channels. The period of 'Umar's ﷺ *Khilafah* is remembered in the history of Islam as an age of expansion, fair administration, stability, and justice, *'Alhamdu li-Llah*

Words and Terms to Remember:

1. *The Hijrah:*
   The migration. Specifically, *Hijrah* means the migration of Rasulullah ﷺ and his *Sahabah* from Makkah to Madinah.

2. *Qudah (Sing. Qadi):*
   Judges. The judge in Islamic Courts who decides according to Islamic Law.

3. *Affiliation:*
   Joining, uniting or attaching to a certain people or group.

4. *Year of the Elephant:*
   The year in which the Christian king of Yemen, Abraha, attacked Makkah.

We Have Learned:

• 'Umar ﷺ appointed *Qudah* in the provinces to conduct judicial administration.

• The *Hijrah* calendar was started under the rule of 'Umar ﷺ.

• 'Umar ﷺ ordered the construction of a number of canals in Egypt and Syria to increase agricultural production.

'Umar ﷺ and Non-Muslims

During the rule of 'Umar ﷺ, Islam had spread to Iraq, Syria, Palestine, Egypt, and some parts of Persia and Central Asia. It was mentioned earlier that only a small number of people in these areas had accepted Islam before their liberation from Byzantine and Persian yoke. Still they wanted Muslims to come to rescue them from the tyrannical rule of the Byzantines and the Sasanids. The support of local Christians was crucial for the victory of the small number of Muslims against the huge armies of their opponents.

Muslims now had a huge non-Muslim population under their rule. They needed to develop new laws to deal with the new situation. Most laws given in the Qur'an or by Rasulullah ﷺ applied to Muslims only. There were general guidelines in the Qur'an and the *Sunnah* of Rasulullah ﷺ about the status of non-Muslims. There was a great need to define relations with non-Muslims and decide about their status in Muslim society. Many specific laws regarding non-Muslims were developed by 'Umar ﷺ which were followed by later generations.

You would recall that the Christians of Jerusalem wanted to surrender to the *Khali-fah* in person. 'Umar ﷺ travelled to Jerusalem for this purpose and assured the freedom of religion to non-Muslims there. He also made sure that the churches and places of worship were not destroyed by Muslims or converted to mosques. The Muslims needed to run the government, and for that they needed to collect taxes from the citizens. Muslims used to pay the *Zakah,* and land tax for this purpose. It was also their duty to fight for the state when it was needed. Non-Muslims were not required to do either of the two.

The Muslims instituted a tax called *Jizyah* for non-Muslims. Only the able-bodied male population paid this tax. In return, the *Khalifah* ensured their personal and family safety, guaranteed them freedom of religion and granted them exemption from going to war to defend the state. But if anybody from the non-Muslims opted to go to war to de-fend the state, he was exempted from this tax. The non-Muslims who accepted to live peacefully in Islamic society and pay *Jizyah* were called *Ahlu-adh-Dhimmah* or *Dhimmis* by the Muslims. *'Ahl* means people and *Dhimmah* means responsibility or obligation. In other words *'Ahl adh-Dhimmah* means people who were the responsibility of the Muslim state for their protection. Muslims were both morally and legally responsible for the safety of non-Muslims.

Islamic laws under 'Umar ﷺ did not discriminate against anyone. Non-Muslims could participate in consultation about governmental affairs, they could also follow their religious laws regarding their personal matters. If a Muslim killed a *Dhimmi*, he would receive the same punishment as of killing a Muslim.

Non-Muslims were allowed to retain the control of their lands. However, they would pay a separate tax on the land they possessed. When Muslims failed to protect the non-Muslims from foreign aggression they re-turned their taxes. You may recall that when Muslims in Syria were in trouble, the fa-mous general Khalid ibn Al-Walid was asked to move to Syria immediately. Before leaving Iraq for Syria, Khalid returned, to non-Muslims of that locality, the *Jizyah* money which he had collected from them earlier.

This treatment to the followers of other religions by Muslims was an exemplary event in history, especially in light of the fact that the people of the area were treated very bad-ly earlier by the Byzantine and the Sasanid rulers. Not only did the Jews and the Christians fight each other, but Christian sects fought among themselves. Islamic authorities played the role of peacemakers and judges in their disputes. Many Jews and Christians came to live under Muslim rule in preference to the rule of their co-religionists.

'Umar ﷺ had a great concern for all the citizens, but he paid special attention to non-Muslims. He felt their payment of *Jizyah* makes the Islamic State, both legally and morally, responsible for their welfare and security. Whenever he came to know that a non-Muslim could not pay his tax because of poverty, he would exempt him and provide for his support from *Bait ul-Mal,* the state treasury.

Even on his deathbed he remembered them and advised his successor saying:

> "Our commitment to non-Muslims must be fulfilled. They should be completely protected against any foreign invasion. They should be treated equally in the courts of law, and no injustice should be done to them. Their taxes should be fair, and no tax should be imposed upon them which they cannot bear."

It was because of this just and fair treatment that most of the people of the area gradually became Muslims.

TAWRAH   BIBLE   QUR'AN

Words and Terms to Remember:

1. *Ahlu-dh-Dhimmah or Dhimmis:*
   Ahlu-dh-Dhimmah means "People under Protection." The non-Muslims living in the Muslim World under the protection of the Islamic State.

2. *Bait ul-Mal:*
   "The House of Wealth," the State Treasury in the Islamic State.

3. *Co-religionists:*
   Those who follow the same religion.

4. *Crucial:*
   Decisive, very important.

5. *To discriminate:*
   To prefer one over other, to distinguish.

6. *Exemption:*
   Freedom from, not paying.

We Have Learned:

- Non-Muslims were given full protection under 'Umar ﷺ.

- Non-Muslims under Muslim protection paid *Jizyah* as tax and they were called *'Ahl al-Dhimmah* or *Dhimmis.*

- Non-Muslims did not participate in war for the protection of the Muslim world.

The Passing of 'Umar &: The Succession of 'Uthman &

The Muslim *'Ummah* lived very happily and peacefully under the leadership of 'Umar &. During the ten years under his rule, Islam grew and prospered. But not everybody was happy with him, particularly those privileged classes who enjoyed life under the rule of the Sasanids and Byzantines.

We have already read of 'Umar's & trip to Jerusalem accompanied by only one attendant. From this story, you can imagine how simple his lifestyle was. Unlike other rulers and kings, he did not employ large numbers of bodyguards and servants to care for him. And, there was no restrictions in carrying arms under the early *Khulafa'*. Therefore, anybody could approach the *Khalifah* with arms.

One day, during the *Salat ul-Fajr,* in the year 23 of *Hijrah* (644 C. E), a man named Feroz attacked 'Umar & with his knife. Feroz came to Madinah from one of the provinces of the old Sasanid Empire and he was a Zoroastrian. 'Umar & suffered from the injury for three days and then died. People asked him on his deathbed about his successor. He then formed a committee of trusted, wise, and experienced Muslims to gather peoples opinions.

He entrusted them with the responsibility of nominating the *Khalifah* within three days of his death.

'Umar & nominated 'Abdur-Rahman ibn 'Awf, 'Uthman ibn 'Affan, 'Ali ibn 'Abi Talib,'Az-Zubair ibn al-'Awwam, Talhah ibn Ubaidullah and Sa'd ibn 'Abi Waqqas & to serve on the committee. These were the wisest and most experienced companions of the Prophet &. He also requested 'Abdur-Rahman & to head the committee, naming his own son, 'Abdullah, to cast a decisive vote if the committee was equally divided on any candidate. 'Umar & also asked Suhaib &, a freed Roman slave to lead prayers for three days until the committee had decided about the *Khalifah.* Being an *'imam* is a very important position in Islam. An *'imam* is not only a leader of the *salah,* but he is also a leader of the community.

'Abdur-Rahman & and other members of the committee consulted most of the people of Madinah and those Muslims who had come to Madinah for pilgrimage. They also kept in mind the choices of governors and people of places distant from Madinah while making the decision, based on their previous discussions with them. It was generally found that most people favored either 'Uthman ⌖ or 'Ali ⌖ to succeed 'Umar ⌖. However, 'Abdur-Rahman ⌖, the leader of the committee, decided that 'Uthman ⌖ should succeed because of his age and experience. 'Uthman ⌖ was more than twenty-five years older than 'Ali ⌖. 'Abdur-Rahman ⌖ declared his *bai'ah* in favor of 'Uthman ⌖, and this was followed later by 'Ali ⌖. Nobody openly protested against this decision. Thus, 'Uthman ⌖ became the third *Khalifah*.

'Uthman ⌖ immediately wrote to governors and other officials, reminding them that his policy would be the same as that of 'Umar ⌖. He wrote to the governors:

> "Allah ⌖ has entrusted you with a heavy responsibility: to be a guardian of your community. Don't be a tax collector only; serve them as much as you can and be fair to everybody. Take interest in the affairs of the common people. Treat the *Dhimmis* fairly. Allah ⌖, has created everybody with fairness and justice and He accepts only what is fair and just. Do not treat the orphans and poor unjustly. Keep in your mind that Allah will punish those who would oppress them."

Have you noticed that the *Khalifah* specially mentioned the non-Muslim *Dhimmis*, the orphans, and the poor? Why do you think that the *Khalifah* specially mentioned fairness and justice for them? Why do you think that the *Khalifah* reminded the governors about justice and fairness again and again? He did so because every powerful man has a tendency to control and exploit the weak. Unless a man is conscious of Allah's Power and Grace, he acts as if he is the most powerful man on earth controlling others; a person, when in a position of power, many times turns out to be an oppressor. That is why the *Khalifah* especially urged his governors to treat the poor and the weak fairly. In fact, Muslim officials did treat everybody fairly. That is why most *Dhimmis* gradually accepted Islam and became a part of the *'Ummah*.

Zarathushtra, or Zoroaster, was founder of the religion named after him as Zoroastrianism. He is believed to have preached his religion in ancient Persia, sometime between 1800 and 700 B.C. The original teachings of Zoroaster emphasized the belief in One God *Ahura Mazda,* and a good moral life.

Later, the religion developed into a dualism showing a constant struggle between Good and Evil. The Zoroastrians became known as fire worshippers because at the center of their worship is the permanent sacred fire which symbolizes the light and the truth.

Zoroastrianism flourished under the Sasanids (226-641 A.D.), when its scriptures, called Yasna, were transcribed in the ancient Persian script. With the advent of Islam and the conquest of Persia by the Muslims in the sixth century, most of the Persians accepted Islam.

The total population of Zoroastrians in the world today numbers only about 200,000, with major concentrations being in India and Iran.

Words and Terms to Remember:

1. *Privilege:*
   A special favor, special rights.

2. *Zoroastrian:*
   A follower of the ancient Persian religion founded by Zoroaster nearly three thousand years ago.

We Have Learned:

- 'Umar ؓ was assassinated by Feroz, a non-Muslim from Persia.

- 'Umar ؓ nominated a committee of six members to consult people and elect the *Khalifah.*

- 'Uthman ؓ, the third *Khalifah,* instructed all governors and other officials to take care of the *Dhimmis,* the poor, and the weak in the society.

The Early Life of 'Uthman ﷺ

'Uthman ﷺ was born in the year 576 C.E., about six years after the Year of the Elephant. Rasulullah ﷺ was only six years old at the time of 'Uthman's ﷺ birth. 'Uthman ﷺ belonged to the influential Bani 'Umayyah clan of the Quraish tribe. 'Uthman ﷺ came from a rich business family and as he grew older he himself became a successful businessman. He was a kind and generous person. He contributed generously in every way he could to help the Prophet ﷺ and the Muslims and those in need. 'Uthman ﷺ also supported many Islamic and social projects. Because of the constant contributions of his wealth in the Path of Allah, he became known as 'Uthman Al-Ghani, or " 'Uthman the Rich and Generous."

During the pre-Islamic days, he was a good friend of 'Abu Bakr ﷺ. It was through him that he came to know of Rasulullah ﷺ. 'Uthman ﷺ accepted Islam at a very early stage of Rasulullah's ﷺ mission. He married Rasulullah's ﷺ second daughter, Ruqayyah ﷺ. People said that 'Uthman ﷺ and Ruqayyah ﷺ were the most beautiful couple in all Makkah. After the death of Ruqayyah ﷺ Rasulullah ﷺ married his other daughter 'Umm Kulthum ﷺ to him. This gives some idea about the love Rasulullah ﷺ had for 'Uthman ﷺ. For this reason he was called *Dhu-n-Nurain,* "the Person with Two Lights."

You will recall that the Muslims were targets for persecution during the early years of Islam. The wealth and influence of 'Uthman ﷺ could not save him from this persecution and victimization. Therefore, when Rasulullah ﷺ instructed some Muslims to migrate to Ethiopia, 'Uthman ﷺ and Ruqayyah ﷺ joined the group. But within a short period, he returned to Makkah having heard that the Muslims had reached an agreement with the Quraish to live peacefully. This was, however, false information. But upon finding this out, 'Uthman ﷺ decided not to return to Ethiopia. He waited in Makkah until the final instruction to migrate to Yathrib (Madinah).

Immediately after his migration to Madinah, Rasulullah ﷺ constructed a big *masjid*. This *masjid* is known as *Masjid an-Nabi* or "Mosque of the Prophet." Muslims from all over the world visit Madinah to pray in this *masjid* and recites *salawat & salaam* to Rasulullah ﷺ. The *masjid* has grown much bigger and fancier with time. At first it was made only of mud bricks and palm trunks, and 'Uthman 🙼 contributed a major share for its construction.

Once, the Muslims of Madinah faced a shortage of fresh water in the city. The only well that could supply enough water belonged to a Jew who charged a very high price for the supply of water. When Rasulullah 🙼 came to know about it, he announced,

> "Whoever among Muslims buys this well and allows everybody to use its water, will be rewarded with Paradise in the Hereafter."

'Uthman 🙼 came forward, bought the well, and dedicated it for the use of all the people of Madinah.

Thus 'Uthman 🙼 was to be counted among the 'Al-'Asharah Al-Mubashsharah or "The Ten Recipients of Good News" who were promised the reward of Paradise by the Prophet 🙼 himself. All of the 'Al-Khulafa' 'Ar-Rashidun were among these ten. In addition to his financial contributions, 'Uthman fought shoulder to shoulder with other Muslims against the enemies of Islam. As was stated in a previous chapter, there was no standing army of the Muslims in those days. Every Muslim man was expected to participate in all activities to spread and defend Islam. Wars against the kuffar and contributions to finance them were a part of these duties. Like all other Muslims, 'Uthman 🙼 did both, except in the case of the Battle of Badr. At that time, his wife Ruqayyah 🙼 was ill and Rasulullah 🙼 asked him to stay

Do you know the modern name of the city of Yathrib? It is Madinah. When Rasulullah 🙼 migrated there, everyone started calling it *Madinat un-Nabi*, "the City of the Prophet." Gradually, the city came to be known as Al-Madinah Al-Munawwarah, the Illuminated City, or simply Madinah.

The Ten Who are in Paradise

'Abdur Rahman ibn 'Awf reports that the Prophet 🙼 had said:

"'Abu Bakr is in Paradise, 'Umar is in Paradise, 'Uthman is in Paradise, 'Ali is in Paradise, Talhah is in Paradise, Zubair is in Paradise, 'Abdur Rahman ibn 'Awf is in Paradise, Sa'd ibn Abi Waqqas is in Paradise, Sa'id ibn Zaid is in Paradise, and 'Ubaida ibn Jarrah is in Paradise."
—*At-Tirmidhi*

home to take care of her. Sadly, his wife Ruqayyah 🙼 died in that illness.

During the period of time known as the "Peace of *Hudaibiyah*" between Muslims and the Makkan Quraish, 'Uthman 🙼 was sent to Makkah by Rasulullah 🙼 to negotiate the entry of Muslims in Makkah for *'Umrah*. At one stage, a rumor was spread that the Quraish had killed 'Uthman 🙼 and Rasulullah 🙼 decided to fight against the Makkans. The rumor, however, proved to be false and there was great rejoicing when he returned to the Muslim camp. 'Uthman 🙼 was greatly admired for his courage and wisdom during this mission.

At the time of the *Tabuk* campaign (9 A.H) against the Byzantine emperor, Rasulullah made a special appeal to all Muslims to contribute generously. 'Uthman ﷺ alone gave enough money to provide ten thousand men with weapons. Rasulullah ﷺ was especially pleased with 'Uthman ﷺ for this gesture and prayed for him.

On another occasion, the people of Madinah faced a severe shortage of food. At that time, one of 'Uthman's ﷺ caravans reached Madinah with food and supplies.

The citizens of Madinah were looking forward to its arrival. Many traders offered to buy the food from 'Uthman ﷺ at a high price and then resell it to the public at higher prices. However, on its arrival, 'Uthman ﷺ refused to sell any of the food, instead he donated the whole caravan free of cost to the people of Madinah.

Words and Terms to Remember:

1. *'Al-Ghani :*
   The Rich, the Generous; this was one of the titles of 'Uthman ﷺ.

2. *'Al-'Asharah Al-Mubashsharah:*
   "The Ten Recipients of Good News." This refers to those ten Companions of Rasulullah ﷺ who were given good news of Paradise in this world.

3. *Dhu-n-Nurain:*
   The Possessor of Two Lights, it was another title of 'Uthman ﷺ.

We Have Learned:

- 'Uthman ﷺ was among the Muslim immigrants to Ethiopia and then to Madinah.

- 'Uthman ﷺ was famous for his wealth and generosity.

- 'Uthman ﷺ was sent by Rasulullah ﷺ to the Quraish to negotiate a peace agreement with the Makkans at the time of the Treaty of *Hudaibiyah*.

The Khalifah of 'Uthman ﷺ : the First

In the beginning, 'Uthman ﷺ continued the same principles and policies that were adop-ted by 'Umar ﷺ. As we know, in a letter written to his governors, 'Uthman ﷺ clearly outlined the policies of his government. In the beginning, he also avoided making changes among high officials in the government. As a result, the Islamic State continued to grow. The lands previously controlled by the Byzantine and Sasanid empires were being captured at equally great speed. Most of the conquered peoples were happy to live under Muslim rule. Everyday more and more people were embracing Islam.

One specific achievement of the rule of 'Uthman ﷺ was the establishment of a navy. During the rule of 'Umar ﷺ, several Muslim leaders suggested to the *Khalifah* that a navy be formed in order to better combat the Byzantine

Empire and defend the coasts of Syria and Egypt from attack. Look at a map of the period and you will notice that by the time of 'Umar ﷺ, Islam had spread from the eastern shores of the Mediterranean and the Red Sea on one side to the Persian Gulf on the other. However, 'Umar ﷺ did not agree with this idea of establishing a navy for Muslims. It is difficult to explain why 'Umar ﷺ did not want to have an Islamic navy. One possible reason may be

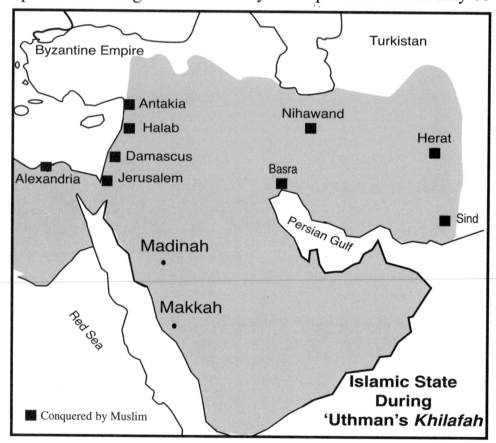

Byzantine Empire

Turkistan

■ Antakia

Nihawand

■ Halab

Herat

■ Damascus

Basra

Alexandria ■ Jerusalem

Madinah
•

Sind

Makkah
•

Red Sea

Persian Gulf

■ Conquered by Muslim

Islamic State During 'Uthman's *Khilafah*

that the Arabs at that time were not familiar with naval warfare. Although it is true that many Arabs during the pre-Islamic days traveled by sea for business purposes, they were never engaged in any naval war and their trading vessels always stayed close to the shore.

With the passage of time, the military needs of the Muslims changed and 'Uthman realized this. Therefore, when some leading Muslims again proposed establishing a Muslim navy, 'Uthman agreed. This was a major development in Islamic history, making Muslims stronger in defending their shores and helping facilitate the conquest of islands such as Crete and Cyprus.

The most important act of the *Khilafah* of 'Uthman was the preparation of the official copy of the Qur'an and its distribution to various parts of the state. It was during the rule of 'Abu Bakr that the Qur'an was collected and put in one volume. However, after this compilation, the Qur'an was kept with the *Khalifah* himself and no other copy was made from it. 'Abu Bakr left this copy of the Qur'an with 'Umar when he nominated him as his successor. At the time of his death, 'Umar left it with his daughter, *'Umm ul-Mu'minin, Hafsah*.

During the rule of 'Uthman, a report came from Azerbaijan that Muslims had developed disagreements on the recitation of the Qur'an. After consulting with leading Muslims, 'Uthman formed a committee of seven members with Zaid ibn Thabit as its head. He was one of the personal scribes of Rasulullah and had compiled the Qur'an during the rule of 'Abu Bakr.

All of the members of the committee, except Zaid, belonged to the Quraish. This was because the Qur'an was revealed in the dialect of the Quraish and these people knew the sound pronunciation and accent of the Qur'an. Some among the members even possessed their personal copies of the Qur'an.

This committee first recompiled the Qur'an in a book form, comparing it with the official copy of 'Abu Bakr. Then they compared this written Qur'an with the recitations of those who had memorized the whole Qur'an. If there was any disagreement about the pronunciation of certain words, they asked the people of the Hijaz who were more familiar with the language and dialect of the Quraish. Thus, under 'Abu Bakr, 'Umar and 'Uthman an authentic version of the Qur'an was officially prepared and distributed throughout the Islamic world.

A unique characteristic of the Qur'an is that unlike other religious scriptures, it has only one version. The Muslim *'Ummah* all over the world follows the same Qur'an. You may find copies of this original version in the museums in the cities of Istanbul in Turki and Tashkent in Uzbekistan.

Words and Terms to Remember:

1. *Authentic:*
   Real, original, without doubt, officially approved.

2. *Dialect:*
   Way of speech special to a group.

3. *Scripture:*
   Sacred writings, religious books that people believe are from God.

4. *'Umm ul-Mu'minin:*
   "Mother of the Believers," a title of the wives of the Prophet ﷺ.

We Have Learned:

- A Muslim navy was first established during the *Khilafah* of 'Uthman ﷺ.

- The Qur'an, in its present form, was officially compiled and distributed throughout the Muslim world under the rule of 'Uthman ﷺ.

- Zaid ibn Thabit ﷺ led the official committees to compile the Qur'an into the final authentic version during the *Khilafah* of both 'Abu Bakr ﷺ and 'Uthman ﷺ.

The Rise of Fitnah: Assassination

In the beginning, the policies carried out by 'Uthman ﷺ worked well. But problems began with some important officials appointed by the *Khalifah*. Some officials did not behave in a responsible manner. Some of them treated the common people unjustly. This happened particularly in lands distant from Madinah, in areas where most people had just recently accepted Islam. You will recall that most distant lands such as Palestine, Egypt, Syria, and Iraq were earlier occupied by the Byzantine or the Sasanids. Muslims helped to free the people of these areas from the tyrannical rule of the emperors. When Muslims established their rule in these areas they also inherited some old problems.

A major problem was the bureaucracy. Bureaucracy means all the people in offices who record and carry out the orders of the gover-nors. These people usually keep their jobs even when the governors change. They are trained to do their jobs and, in a big government, the head may not be able to keep track of everything the bureaucracy does.

As Muslim rule extended, they took advantage of the talents of the trained bureaucrats of the previous imperial governments. Although many of these people became Muslims, they had never known Rasulullah ﷺ. They never lived in Madinah during his blessed rule. So the only example of government that they had known was that of the Persians or Byzantines. Many of these people were not as honest or generous as they should have been.

Another major problem was the increase in wealth. Rasulullah ﷺ had foreseen that great wealth would be bad for the *'Ummah*. When Syria was captured by the Muslims, they found a land overflowing in wealth and prosperity. It is said that 'Umar ﷺ cried when he saw such enormous wealth. Someone asked the *Khalifah*, "Why are you crying, while we have captured so much?" 'Umar ﷺ replied, "I am afraid that one day this wealth will ruin our *'Ummah!* It is very difficult not to be tempted with this kind of wealth. And when someone is tempted, he can be corrupted easily."

'Umar ﷺ was very careful and strict about the activities of his governors and other officials in different parts of the Islamic territory. Whenever he found any trace of corruption by any official, he would replace him. Therefore, no corrupt official existed anywhere under his government and the people were very happy. But after his death even some of his officials became relaxed and neglected their duties.

'Uthman ﷺ was an extremely gentle and very humble person and he was loved by the people for this. However, he was not as strong a leader as 'Umar ﷺ was. Islam was spreading to many lands and 'Uthman ﷺ was not always able to take strong action against the corrupt officials in his government. Therefore, after his first few years in power, he started to receive complaints against some of his governors and other officials in distant parts of his realm. On the basis of these complaints, he changed the governors of the provinces of Kufah (in Iraq) and Egypt. But this did not satisfy many people in those areas and his government came under increasing pressure.

Some governors under him grew very powerful in the regions they governed. Among them were Mu'awiyah ibn 'Abi Sufyan who was the governor of Syria and 'Amr ibn 'Al-'As, the governor of Egypt. Most of these powerful governors and officials came from the 'Umayyad clan of the Quraish, the clan of 'Uthman ﷺ himself.

The 'Umayyads were responsible for insuring the comfort of the pilgrims during the annual pilgrimage in pre-Islamic Arabia. They also had extensive business connections outside Arabia. They were also relatively wealthier than the other clans in Makkah. Because of their experience as administrators and businessmen, 'Uthman's predecessor, 'Umar ﷺ, nominated many of them to high positions in the government. These governors were far away from Madinah and the *Khalifah*. The power and wealth of their new positions may have corrupted some of them. They became careless and lost some of their fairness and simplicity. Some of them forgot the humility of character that was found in the early years of the *Khilafah*.

Since 'Uthman ﷺ himself came from the clan of Banu 'Umayyah, many people started to believe that he did not want to take action against his corrupt relatives. Some even started to blame 'Uthman ﷺ himself for his own wealth, ignoring the fact that he was a rich man before he became *Khalifah*. This created a tension between the 'Umayyad clan and others among the Muslims.

On various occasions, 'Uthman ﷺ answered the people about the complaints he received against himself and his officials. He said that he was a wealthy businessman long before he became the *Khalifah*. He had contributed generously and continuously to the work of Islam. He also explained that he was never involved in corrupt and unjust activities. People believed him and most of them withdrew their complaints against the *Khalifah*. But some other people provoked by Islam's enemies remained hostile and continued to create more *fitnah* and hostilities.

Once a number of people came to Madinah from Kufah, Basrah, and Egypt, complaining against the governors in their territories. 'Uthman listened to them carefully and assured them that he would take action against any corrupt official. On hearing this, the group of complainers left Madinah apparently satisfied with the *Khalifah's* response. On their way out of the city, something mysterious happened. They found a person who had carried a secret letter from the *Khalifah* to his governors. This letter commanded them to kill these people when they returned home.

This letter was, in fact, a forgery by an enemy of Islam named 'Abdullah ibn Sabah, who sought to stir up trouble in the Muslim *'Ummah*. Within a short time, the group returned and surrounded the house of the *Khalifah* in Madinah. They also produced a letter with the official seal of the *Khalifah* to him. 'Uthman denied the charges. But they refused to listen to the *Khalifah* and they killed him. It was the 34th year of *Hijrah* or 656 C.E.

'Ali, was proclaimed the *Khalifah* by some leading *Sahabah*. This was done on the basis of opinion gathered during the election of 'Uthman. 'Ali was then most people's second choice. 'Ali now was the overwhelming choice of the community.

Words and Terms to Remember:

1. *Fitnah:*
   Sedition, mischief, afflication. In Islamic history it refers to the sad events which led to the martyrdom of 'Uthman and the weakening of the Islamic State.

We Have Learned:

- Many high officials in the government of 'Uthman belonged to the Banu 'Umayyah clan of the Quraish tribe, which was also 'Uthman's clan.

- 'Uthman denied the charges of corruption against him.

- 'Uthman was assassinated in the 34th year of the *Hijrah,* and 'Ali was elected to take the position of *Khalifah.*

The Early Life of 'Ali ☙

'Ali ☙ was the first cousin of Rasulullah ☙. However, 'Ali's relationship to Rasulullah ☙ was much closer than just being a cousin. He was thirty years younger than the Prophet ☙ and was brought up by him like a son. 'Ali's ☙ father, Abu Talib, a powerful and respected Quraish leader, was poor and had many children. So Rasulullah ☙ took 'Ali ☙ into his household at the age of four. From then on 'Ali ☙ became a member of the family of Rasulullah ☙.

'Ali ☙ was only ten years old when Rasulullah ☙ began to receive *Wahi* (Revelations) from Allah ☙. When Rasulullah ☙ invited his close friends to Islam, 'Ali ☙ was the first one among the youth to accept Islam. From the beginning he devotedly served Rasulullah ☙, actively participating in the activities of building the new *'Ummah.*

At the time of *Hijrah,* 'Ali ☙ was twenty three years old. After receiving instructions from Allah ☙, Rasulullah ☙ prepared to move to Madinah. But his enemies were planning to kill him, and Rasulullah ☙ needed to foil his enemies' plan. On the night of his departure from Makkah, he asked 'Ali ☙ to sleep in his bed under his cloak, so that if anyone looked in from outside they would believe Rasulullah ☙ was sleeping there.

Rasulullah ☙ also needed to leave 'Ali ☙ behind in order to return the money and goods that people had deposited with him. Although most of the people of Makkah were not yet Muslims, they trusted Rasulullah ☙ as *'Al-Amin,* the trustworthy person. They had deposited their money and valuables with Rasulullah ☙, trusting that their wealth would be secure with him.

According to a pre-arranged plan, Rasulullah ☙ left Makkah with 'Abu Bakr ☙ and 'Ali ☙ went to sleep in his bed. The Makkan enemies were outwitted and Rasulullah ☙ arrived at Madinah safely. After returning the depositors' money, 'Ali ☙ joined Rasulullah ☙ a few days later. Within a year after *Hijrah,* 'Ali ☙ married Fatimah ☙, the youngest daughter of Rasulullah ☙. The Prophet ☙ blessed their marriage and it was in turn, a blessing for everyone. 'Ali ☙ and Fatimah ☙ had a number of children including Hasan ☙, Husain ☙, and Zainab ☙.

As a young man, 'Ali ☙ was famous for his bravery and fighting skills. One common practice of the wars in those days was to have a few individuals engage in combat before the beginning of general battle. Usually, the parties used to send their best fighters into these individual combats. 'Ali ﷺ represented the Muslims on a number of occasions and he won everytime. That is how he earned the title 'Asadullah or the "Lion of Allah."

'Ali ﷺ was very intelligent and learned the skill of reading and writing in his life. Infact, he was the person who first wrote down the rules of Arabic grammer. Therefore, he became one of the early official scribes (Katib) of the Qur'an for Rasulullah ﷺ. He used to write the Revelations immediately after they were revealed. He also wrote a number of letters and documents representing the person of Rasulullah ﷺ and the Muslim 'Ummah. He is also reported to have written the Treaty of Hudaibiyah (7 A.H.) between the Muslims and the Quraish. Because of his distinguished services to Islam, 'Ali ﷺ was also one of those given the good news of being assured paradise by the Prophet ﷺ.

During the life of the Prophet ﷺ, 'Ali ﷺ was as close to him as a son or brother. He helped and served him in every way. He also absorbed from him the deepest spiritual teachings and many details of the Sunnah only available to the closest of the Companions. From the moment of the passing away of Rasulullah ﷺ, many people believed that only 'Ali ﷺ had the right to be Khalifah. However, he refused to cause division amongst the 'Ummah, and he sat quietly as an advisor to the first three Khulafa' until his turn came to rule.

'Ali ﷺ is known for his bravery, chivalry, nobility, and learning. He was a generous victor, an intelligent advisor, and a devoted Muslim.

Words and Terms to Remember:

1. *Asadullah:*
   "The Lion of Allah." This title was given to 'Ali ﷺ by Rasulullah ﷺ.

2. *Chivalry:*
   Bravery, qualities of a brave fighter, generosity in war.

We Have Learned:

* When Rasulullah ﷺ made *Hijrah* to Madinah, he chose 'Ali ﷺ to stay behind him and sleep in his bed.

* 'Ali ﷺ earned the title 'Asadullah for his bravery and fighting skills.

* 'Ali ﷺ married Fatimah ﷺ, the youngest daughter of Rasulullah ﷺ.

The Khilafah of 'Ali ﷺ

After becoming the *Khalifah,* 'Ali ﷺ faced two difficult tasks. One was the problem of discontent that some people had for some of the governors in the various provinces. It has already been mentioned how this discontent eventually led to the assassination of the previous *Khalifah,* 'Uthman ﷺ. This tragic event was made worse by the stay of the rebels in Madinah who wanted to make sure that their complaints were taken care of. The assassination of 'Uthman ﷺ created the second major problem for 'Ali ﷺ. Some *Sahabah* became so much disturbed by the murder that they demanded immediate punishment of those responsible for 'Uthman's ﷺ assassination.

'Ali ﷺ had to decide which problem to address first. Public opinion in Madinah was divided. Some people were extremely angered at the killing of the aged and pious *Khalifah;* they demanded that the new *Kha-lifah* punish the killers immediately. Others wanted 'Ali ﷺ to act more cautiously by addressing the problems of discontent first and then punishing those who had murdered 'Uthman ﷺ. " The two issues cannot be treated separately," they argued. 'Ali ﷺ himself seemed to favor the latter course. He wanted to punish the

killers for taking the law into their hands and killing the *Khalifah* unjustly. But he also wanted to strengthen his own position before taking any action that would weaken *Khilafah.* He also wanted to find out about the real complaints from the people and take necessary action.

However, before he could make a decision as to which course to follow, the situation deteriorated into confusion. Some people in Madinah started a movement to force 'Ali ﷺ to punish the killers immediately. Some of them even went outside Madinah together public opinion in favor of their view. *'Umm ul-Mu'minin* 'A'ishah ﷺ, was not in Madinah at the time of the assassination of 'Uthman ﷺ. She had gone to Makkah to perform the *Hajj* and had stayed there for some time.

When 'A'ishah ﷺ learned that 'Uthman ﷺ was assassinated, she became very distressed. The reports reaching her suggested that 'Ali ﷺ was not prepared to take any action against the killers. She and several other *Sahabah* decided to fight 'Ali ﷺ if he failed to move against the rebels. Those who supported this view gathered around 'A'ishah ﷺ. She was supported by many prominent *Sahabah,* including

Talhah ﷺ and Zubair ﷺ. 'A'ishah ﷺ had great influence among the Muslims. She had been delegated by Rasulullah ﷺ to teach people their *Din*. Also she was the daughter of 'Abu Bakr ﷺ and was the foremost among the *'Umm ul-Mu'minin.*

On his part, the new *Khalifah* issued orders to replace the governors in the various provinces. In some cases, however, 'Ali ﷺ retained the previous governors at the request of the local population. Some governors left their positions without protest. In some other cases, governors openly defied the *Khalifah's* order. This helped to further instigate civil war among the *'Ummah.*

Meanwhile, supporters of 'A'ishah ﷺ advised that she move to Basrah, a town in the south of Iraq. There, she and her supporters could expect more support for their cause. Therefore, 'A'ishah ﷺ moved to Basrah, and, in a short battle, defeated supporters of 'Ali ﷺ there. Her supporters also executed those in Basrah who had supported the killing of 'Uthman ﷺ. 'A'ishah ﷺ, along with Talhah ﷺ and Zubair ﷺ, started gathering their supporters to avenge the murder of 'Uthman ﷺ.

On hearing this, 'Ali ﷺ gathered an army and rushed to Basrah. He did not want 'A'ishah ﷺ to take the law into her own hands. After reaching Basrah he went to negotiate with 'A'ishah ﷺ. Now we come to a cloudy and misunderstood event in our history. The two met in negotiation. It is said that they came to an agreement that

would spare any loss of blood. However, the two armies were facing each other, ready for battle. During this crucial period, some of the murderers of 'Uthman ﷺ, who were in the ranks of both the forces, started the fight before 'Ali ﷺ and 'A'ishah ﷺ could reach a compromise.

In the battle, 'Ali's forces scored a victory. Many of the supporters of 'A'ishah ﷺ were killed and she herself was captured. But according to her status as *'Umm ul-Mu'minin*, she was given proper respect and was escorted to her home in Madinah. The government of 'Ali ﷺ also did not stop the stipend which she received from the *Bait ul-Mal*. 'A'ishah ﷺ later felt a great remorse in waging the war. She repented to Allah ﷻ and sought His forgiveness. In this battle she rode in a litter on the back of a camel and so the battle between 'Ali ﷺ and 'A'ishah ﷺ became known as the Battle of Camel *(Jamal)*. This occurred in 36 A.H. or 656 C.E.

This was not the end of the problems of 'Ali ﷺ. Some of the replaced governors became involved in making plots against his rule. Some of them had enjoyed considerable influence in pre-Islamic Arabia. Towards the end of the mission of Rasulullah ﷺ they had become Muslims and played active roles in the spread of Islam. This improved their status in the society. Their leader, Mu'awiyah Ibn 'Abi Sufyan ﷺ, was governor of Syria. He ruled Syria for more than twenty years. The deposed governors of some of the other provinces gathered around

Mu'awiyah ﷺ and threatened the rule of 'Ali ﷺ.

'Ali ﷺ knew well that any military move against them would mean a massive loss of life. However, after bringing the situation in Basrah under control, 'Ali ﷺ moved his capital from Madinah to Kufah, a city between Basrah and Syria. He made this change because he thought it would be easier for him to control Syria and Iraq from Kufah, rather than from Madinah, and a large portion of the population of Iraq supported his cause.

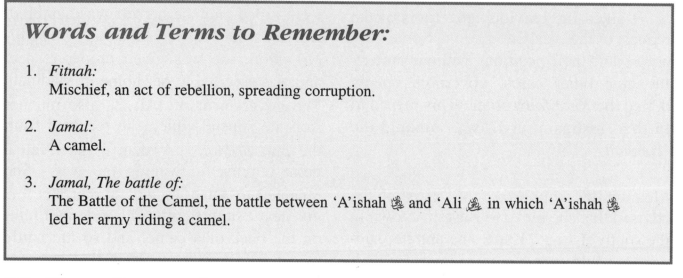

Words and Terms to Remember:

1. *Fitnah:*
   Mischief, an act of rebellion, spreading corruption.

2. *Jamal:*
   A camel.

3. *Jamal, The battle of:*
   The Battle of the Camel, the battle between 'A'ishah ﷺ and 'Ali ﷺ in which 'A'ishah ﷺ led her army riding a camel.

We Have Learned:

- After 'Uthman's ﷺ assassination some people of Madinah demanded immediate punishment of his killers, others wanted the new *Khalifah* to replace the corrupt governors first.

- 'A'ishah ﷺ fought 'Ali ﷺ in the "Battle of the Camel" and she was defeated.

- 'Ali ﷺ moved the seat of government from Madinah to Kufah.

The Clash at Siffin

When 'Ali ﷺ arrived at a place called Siffin in Syria, he noted the presence of Mu'awiyah's ﷺ army. Without rushing into an armed confrontation, 'Ali ﷺ tried to discuss the problem with Mu'awiyah ﷺ directly. But Mu'awiyah ﷺ was not prepared for any discussion. He demanded immediate punishment of the killers of 'Uthman ﷺ.

However, 'Ali ﷺ had already made it clear that the matter of the murder would be taken into consideration only after Mu'awiyah ﷺ and the other rebels recognized him as the *Khalifah*. In the eyes of 'Ali ﷺ, Mu'awiyah ﷺ could not demand anything of him until and unless he declared his *bai'ah* to him. Mu'awiyah ﷺ still refused to pledge his allegiance to 'Ali

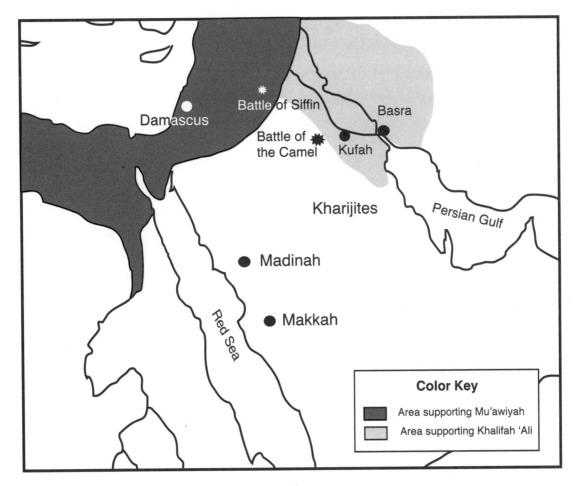

Damascus

Battle of Siffin

Basra

Battle of the Camel

Kufah

Kharijites

Persian Gulf

Madinah

Makkah

Red Sea

Color Key

Area supporting Mu'awiyah

Area supporting Khalifah 'Ali

. All efforts of peaceful solutions failed and finally the two forces plunged into a battle.

In this three-day battle, the forces of the *Khalifah* defeated the rebel army under Mu'awiyah . Mu'awiyah and his army was about to flee from the battlefield when some of his close associates advised him to seek negotiation through a clever plan. They knew that such a noble person like 'Ali would not reject any proposal for peace. They also knew that this would gain time to regroup their forces even if the negotiation failed. So Mu'awiyah ordered that pages of the Holy Qur'an be stuck on the spears of his front rank soldiers. Seeing this, 'Ali halted his army's advance and awaited the negotiations. 'Ali did not want to shed blood anymore. He nominated 'Abu Musa 'Al-'Ash'ari , the ex-governor of Kufah, to negotiate on his behalf. 'Amr Ibn 'Al-'As , an experienced commander and administrator, came forward to represent Mu'awiyah . As soon as 'Ali accepted the idea of negotiation, some of his supporters protested very strongly. "There is nothing to negotiate in this matter. Mu'awiyah is wrong in waging war against the *Khalifah*. In waging war against the *Khalifah* and against Allah, he has deviated from Islam and, therefore, he should be punished. We must not negotiate with him about anything!" they argued. However, 'Ali tried to keep to his word, ignored this group's opinion and went ahead with negotiations.

This group created further problems for 'Ali . Those who opposed the idea of negotiation with Mu'awiyah now turned against 'Ali himself. They thought 'Ali had committed a serious sin by agreeing to talk with Mu'awiyah . This group took up arms against 'Ali and his loyal supporters. These people are known in history as the *Khawarij* or Kharijites.

Meanwhile negotiations continued while 'Ali consolidated his power in Kufah and Mu'awiyah strengthened his position in Syria. This took several months. Finally, it was decided that there would be a *shura* on the office of *Khalifah* and that neither 'Ali nor Mu'awiyah would be considered for the office. The one chosen as *Khalifah* would then address all the problems of the *'Ummah*.

According to the agreement reached, the representative of 'Ali made a declaration in a big public gathering saying, "I declare 'Ali to have renounced his position as the *Khalifah* of the Muslims." However, Mu'awiyah's party secretly decided at the last minute to use 'Ali's resignation to their advantage. 'Amr ibn 'Al-'As , the representative of Mu'awiyah made a statement to the same gathering that, "We accept the deposition of 'Ali and declare that Mu'awiyah will be *Khalifah* in his place." This, of course, was not accepted by 'Ali's supporters, who realizing they had been tricked, called off the talks. Both parties again came to the verge of war. During the period of negotiation, Mu'awiyah gathered a fresh army.

The failure of negotiation angered not only 'Ali's ﷺ supporters, but the *Kharijites* as well. This group was now convinced that all the parties who participated in the negotiation process had committed a sinful act and must be punished. They decided to kill not only 'Ali ﷺ but also Mu'awiyah ﷺ and 'Amr ibn 'Al-'As ﷺ. However, the Kharijites lacked any army to challenge both 'Ali ﷺ and Mu'awiyah ﷺ in the field. Therefore, they assigned a few individuals to go and assassinate the three persons. 'Amr ﷺ escaped the attempt unharmed, Mu'awiyah ﷺ was wounded but survived. 'Ali ﷺ, was not so fortunate, and a Kharijite named 'Ibn Muljim took a dagger and mortally wounded the great Muslim as he offered his Fajr prayer in the year 40 A. H. or 661 C.E. This ended the historical period of *'Al-Khulafa' Ar-Rashidun* or the Rightly Guided Caliphs. We shall analyze some of the ideas related to their rule in the last two lessons.

Words and Terms to Remember:

1. *Kharijites (sing. Khwarij)*
   Literally, "the Seceders". A Muslim sect which arose in opposition to both 'Ali ﷺ and Mu'awiyah ﷺ after the Battle of Siffin, they opposed 'Ali's ﷺ compromise.

2. *Negotiation:*
   Discussing some issue , confer with others to reach an agreement.

We Have Learned:

- After initial defeat, some advisors of Mu'awiyah ﷺ advised him to seek reconciliation through negotiation with 'Ali ﷺ.

- The *Khawarij,* who were originally supporters of 'Ali ﷺ, protested against the idea of negotiation with Mu'awiyah ﷺ.

- After the failure of negotiations the Kharijites decided to kill 'Ali ﷺ, Mu'awiyah ﷺ, and 'Amr Ibn 'Al-'As ﷺ.

The Contributions of 'Ali ؓ

From the beginning, the *Khilafah* of 'Ali ؓ was torn by the *Fitnah* of division and civil war. This meant that there was little he could do in terms of improving the condition of the Islamic State. Muslim armies were diverted inward, fighting among themselves, instead of fighting their enemies. Thus, during the rule of 'Ali ؓ there was little territorial expansion. He had almost no impact on the internal administration of the Islamic State because most of the governors that he appointed to manage the various provinces were disposed by Mu'awiyah ؓ and his supporters.

It was during the *Khilafah* of 'Ali ؓ that the *'Ummah* split into groups that had different ideas about what it means to be a Muslim. The first group to split away were the *Khawarij*. Although they accepted the Five Pillars of Islamic belief, they developed some ideas about sin that were quite different from the accepted view. They were also very violent in their opposition to those people who did not accept their views. The *Khawarij* eventually died out as a group over the centuries.

Another group that was to emerge as a result of the civil war over the *Khalifah* were the *Shi'ah* 'Ali (the Supporters of 'Ali) or simply the *Shi'ah*. They were originally those who supported the claim of 'Ali ؓ and, after his death, the claims of his two sons, Hasan and Husain ؓ. But after their deaths, the *Shi'ah* began to develop religious ideas about the *'Ahl ul-Bait* (the Family of Rasulullah ﷺ that were distinct from the majority of *Sunni* Muslims.

This group believes that 'Ali ؓ was supposed to be the true successor of Rasulullah ﷺ and that 'Abu Bakr ؓ, 'Umar ؓ, and 'Uthman ؓ had usurped this right from him. The *Shi'ah* also believe that only a descendent of Rasulullah ﷺ, through 'Ali ؓ and Fatimah ؓ, could be an *'Imam* and has a right to govern over the *'Ummah*. Over time, the *Shi'ah* split into several sects, as each one supported a different descendent of Rasulullah ﷺ. The majority of *Shi'ah* today belong to the *'Ithna 'Ashriyyah* (Twelvers; they follow the line of the Twelve *'Imams* who were direct descendants of Rasulullah ﷺ through Fatimah ؓ and 'Ali ؓ) and their basic beliefs are close to the majority of *Sunni* Muslims. The *Shi'ah* are mainly to be found in Iran, Iraq, Lebanon, and some parts of South Asia.

The majority of Muslims were made up of those who neither joined the *Khawarij* nor the *Shi'ah*. The group became known as the *'Ahl us-Sunnah wa-l-Jama'ah* (The People of the *Sunnah* and the Community) or simply the *Sunni*. The *Sunnis* accept the *Sunnah* of Rasulullah, *'Al-Khulafa' Ar-Rashidun,* and the *Sahabah.* They accept the decisions which the *'Ummah* took for the succession of the *Khulafa'*. They honor all of the *'Al-Khulafa' 'Ar-Rashidun* and all the *'Ahl ul-Bait* . The *Sunnis* love the family of the Prophet ﷺ, but do not believe it has any special religious or political authority. The overwhelming majority of Muslims belong to the *'Ahl As-Sunnah wa-l-Jama'ah*. Both *Shi'ah* and *Sunni* have com-mon beliefs and it is only the succession to Rasulullah ﷺ that they differ about. All the Muslims are like one body and in spite of some differences in their views, we must learn to respect each other and live together in peace.

Despite all of this confusion and chaos, 'Ali ؏ made great impact on the history of Islam. He was well known for being an outstanding *mu'min* whose love and devotion to Rasulullah ﷺ had no equal. 'Ali ؏ had always set his sights on the Next World and strove diligently in that direction. This attitude was probably a result of his having lived as a member of the family of Rasulullah ﷺ. Like the other three *Khulafa'*, 'Ali ؏ was a great soldier and had a deep insight into the message and meaning of Islam. 'Ali's ؏ knowledge of Islam was so highly respected that even 'Abu Bakr ؏ and 'Umar ؏ used to come to him for advice during their *Khilafah*. In fact 'Umar ؏ had once said, "If it were not for 'Ali, I would have been ruined."

Not only was 'Ali ؏ *a hafiz* of the *Qur'an,* but he could relate the exact moment when any given *'ayah* was revealed to Rasulullah ﷺ. It was 'Ali ؏ who drafted the famous Treaty of Hudaibiyah between the Muslims and the Quraish. 'Ali ؏ was also the first person to set the rules of grammar for the Arabic language in writing. A large body of the letters, *khutab,* and sayings of 'Ali ؏ were compiled in the book *Nahju-l-Balaghah.* This work shows the great literary wisdom and speaking skills that 'Ali ؏ was blessed with.

Words and Terms to Remember:

1. *'Ithna 'Ashriyyah:*
   The Twelvers or the Followers of Twelve Imans. The majority branch of Shi'i Islam who believe in 'Ali ﷺ and his eleven successors as the twelve *Imans*.

2. *The Khawarij (The Kharijites):*
   Literally, "the seceders". A sect which arose in opposition to both Mu'awiyah ﷺ and 'Ali ﷺ.

3. *Khutab (sing. Khutbah):*
   Sermon, lecture, speech.

4. *Usurp:*
   To take something without right; getting something by force and not by law.

5. *'Ahl As-Sunnah wa-l-Jama'ah, or the Sunni:*
   The majority of the Muslims who believe in all of the four caliphs as Al-*Khulafa' Ar-Rashidun* and a system of *shura*.

6. *Shi'ah 'Ali or Shi'ah:*
   The party of 'Ali; those who believe 'Ali ﷺ and his children were the legitimate successors to Rasulullah ﷺ..

We Have Learned:

- Ali ﷺ was an outstanding *Sahabi* of Rasulullah ﷺ, known for his courage, knowledge, and faithfulness.

- The *Shi'ah* believe that only a descendant of Rasulullah ﷺ through the line of 'Ali and Fatimah ﷺ could be an *'Imam* and a successor to Rasulullah ﷺ.

- All the Muslims are like one body and must respect each other and work together for the cause of Islam.

70

Al-Khulafa' ar-Rashidun: Their Importance

The rule of the first four *Khulafa'* is called *Al-Khilafah Ar-Rashidah,* "The Rightly Guided *Khilafah.*" *Al-Khilafah Ar-Rashidah* lasted for about thirty years; it ended with the martyrdom of 'Ali ☙ and the beginning of the rule of Mu'awiyah ☙, the first *Umay-yad Khalifah.*

All the four successors to Rasulullah ☙ are called *Al-Khulafa' Ar-Rashidun* or "The Rightly Guided Caliphs." Their rule is regarded as the golden age of Islam. In their persons they were the best examples of Islam in practice and in their political rule they were guided by the teachings of the Qur'an and the *Sunnah* of Rasulullah ☙. Many later Muslim rulers followed the example of the *Khulafa'* and their rule contributed to many great achievements in the arts and sciences but they could never reach the moral and religious standards of this early period of the rule of the four *Khulafa'.*

They were specially trained for the task of leadership in the company of Rasulullah ☙. They had developed in their characters the same characteristics of simplicity, sincerity, and piety as Rasulullah ☙ himself poss-essed. All the four *Khulafa'* were the closest *Sahabah* of Rasulullah ☙ and received their personal trainings under his guidance. They accepted Islam at an early stage and remained faithful to Allah ☙ and His Messenger ☙ during all difficulties and trials.

The *Khulafa'* were the most knowledgeable people of their time. Islam is a religion of knowledge, and Rasulullah ☙ was sent by Allah ☙ as a teacher. The *Khulafa'* received their knowledge directly from Rasulullah ☙ and became the best teachers in their own turn.

> 'Abu Bakr ☙ was well known for his knowledge of the Qur'an, *Tafsir, and Fiqh,* and was able to interpret the events of his time in the light of his knowledge of Islam.
>
> 'Umar ☙ had not only knowledge of Islam but a great insight into the understanding of the issues. Rasulullah ☙ said, "If there was to be a prophet after me, it would have been 'Umar."
>
> 'Uthman ☙ was one of the literate people even during *Jahiliyyah* and became one of the writers of the Qur'an as it was revealed. His special interest was in the Qur'an and he finalized its compilation and safeguarded its final collection.
>
> " 'Ali is to me as Harun is to Musa," said Rasulullah ☙ of 'Ali ☙. He further said, "I am the city of knowledge and 'Ali is its gate."

71

The *Khulafa'* did not only have the knowledge of Islam but they also practiced what they had learned. They were the best examples of Islamic *'Akhlaq* (morals and manners). They spent their days in the service of the *'Ummah* and their nights in prayers. Though they were among the ten who were promised *Jannah,* in this life they feared Allah ﷻ, cried before Him for any possible faults and sins, and strove to do Allah's ﷻ Will. They were modest and kind in their personal relations and strong and courageous in battles for Islam. They led very modest lives but were most generous in helping the cause of Islam and helping other needy people. They were equally fair and just in their dealings with others.

The *Khulafa'* were guided by the Qur'an and the *Sunnah* of Rasulullah ﷺ in their minutest details. Even if they felt that a changed situation demanded a fresh approach, they trusted the *Sunnah* of Rasulullah ﷺ over their own judgment. Later experience showed the *'Ummah* how right their decisions were to follow the *Sunnah* of Rasulullah ﷺ.

Islamic history has seen many remarkable rulers and it recorded their great achievements. Their greatness of character is also judged by the standards of how closely they followed the personal life and social responsibilities of these earliest Muslim rulers. There are many special characteristics of this period that makes it so unique not only in the history of Islam but the history of the world. The greatness of the period is, in fact, due to the special charac-

ters of these *Khulafa'*. We shall discuss below, their unique characteristics which make this period the greatest in Islamic history and their personal characters as some of the noblest and greatest in human history.

The Qur'an describes the characteristics of those sincere *Sahabah* of Rasulullah ﷺ who accepted Islam and followed the Prophet ﷺ throughout their lives:

> "The true believers are those who believe in Allah and His Messenger, and afterward never doubt and strive with their wealth and with their lives in the path of Allah; such are the sincere ones."
> (*'Al-Hujurat* 49:15)

They had a great history of self-sacrifice for the cause of Islam and on every occasion came up with everything they possessed to sacrifice on the call of Rasulullah ﷺ and for the cause of Islam.

'Uthman ﷺ was a rich merchant. He never missed an occasion to use his wealth

On the occasion of the battle of *Tabuk* , Rasulullah ﷺ invited all the *Sahabah* to come forward with support for this very important campaign. 'Umar ﷺ offered half of everything of what he possessed. 'Abu Bakr ﷺ brought everything he had. Rasulullah ﷺ asked him, "Did you leave anything for your family?" He replied, 'Yes! O Rasulullah ﷺ, I have left the name of Allah and His Messenger for them."

for the well being of the *'Ummah*. 'Ali ﷺ had very little financial resources initially. Later in Madinah, his income increased but it did not change his lifestyle. He would give all his wealth to the needy and the poor and often went to sleep hungry at night.

Because of their sacrifices and sincerity they had the trust of the 'Ummah. They loved the Messenger ﷺ, were faithful to his message, were prepared to sacrifice for Islam and the well-being of the 'Ummah. They were the best examples after Rasulullah ﷺ of Islam in practice.

Al-Khulafa' Ar-Rashidun led very simple lives. They wore simple clothes, had no palaces, ate very simple food, and had no personal bodyguards to protect them. They came to the Masjid five times every day and were easily available to any common person all the time. They did not expect any special treatment from others. No one could distinguish between a Khalifah and a common person when they sat or walked with others.

Their acceptance of the position of the Kha-lifah made them even more conscious of their responsibilities as rulers. They were elected Khulafa' against their own wishes. They believed there were other people more qualified for the task and they were afraid in case they were not able to fulfill their responsibilities well and receive Allah's punishment.

'Umar ﷺ was so concerned about the well-being of the people, he would himself go out to inquire about their needs and preferred to fulfill them himself personally. He walk-ed around in the market and

> 'Abu Bakr ﷺ, thinking of his task used to cry and say, " I wish I were a stone free from the burden of Khilafah."

neighborhoods to find out about the needs of the people.

'Umar ﷺ said, "I will regard myself lucky in the Sight of Allah, if I fulfill my responsibilities of the Khilafah in such a way that

> Once 'Umar ﷺ saw a poor Bedouin whose wife was expecting a child. He brought his wife to help the lady in child birth and himself carried the sacks of flour and other needed supplies. His servant 'Aslam asked him to help him carry the sacks but 'Umar ﷺ refused. He believed that as a Khalifah he had a personal responsibility to help every citizen himself.

people sleep comfortably in their homes. I will deem myself unlucky if people are forced to come to me for their needs."

The Khulafa' regarded themselves responsible for all the citizens of the state and showed no favors to their family members and personal friends.

The life and example of Al-Khulafa' Ar-Rashidun shows us that to build a true Islamic society we must first build our

> Once 'Ali's brother, 'Aqil ﷺ, approached him for some advance money from the Bait ul-Mal. 'Ali ﷺ refused his request. 'Aqil ﷺ became so annoyed with 'Ali ﷺ that he went over to his rival Mu'awiyah ﷺ. 'Ali ﷺ did not change his mind. He felt Bait ul-Mal is the trust of the 'Ummah and his family has no special rights on it."

Islamic character. Islam is not something to be preached to others, but a way of life to be first practiced by those who profess this religion. A true Muslim is one who follows the Qur'an, the *Sunnah,* the example of *Sahabah* and other pious ancesters, and inspires others by his noble example, and not one who expects others to practice what he as a Muslim believes.

Words and Terms to Remember:

1. *Characteristics:*
   Special traits, marks and qualities of something.

2. *Constitutional Ruler:*
   A ruler who works according to the law of the land.

3. *Dictator:*
   A ruler who has absolute power; a ruler who rules by his own authority.

4. *Responsibility:*
   Condition of being responsible, trustworthy, answerable.

5. *Scribe:*
   A writer; a person who copies literature professionally.

We Have Learned:

- The first four Rightly Guided Caliphs are called *Al-Khulafa' Ar-Rashidun.*

- These *Khulafa'* were the first to accept Islam and received their training from Rasulullah ﷺ.

- Their characters are the best example after the *Sunnah* of Rasulullah ﷺ for us to follow in private life and public affairs.

Al-Khilafah ar-Rashidah: A Model Islamic State

We have seen in the previous chapter how unique the characters of *Al-Khulafa' Ar-Rasidun* were. The institution of *Al-Khilafah Ar-Rashidah* was also a unique system of government. It introduced new principles of government which did not exist in the ancient world and have only recently been introduced in some of the modern states of the world.

The first principle of *Al-Khilafah Ar-Rashidah* was the Islamic *shura,* the principle of mutual consultation. The *shura* is one of the central principles of Islam. The *shura* means we must decide everything, be it personal or social by discussing it with those people who are concerned with the matter.

> Allah ﷻ said about Muslims in the Qur'an, "...that their affairs are decided by mutual consultation...." (*'Ash-Shura* 42:38)

The Qur'an calls it a characteristic of all Muslims to consult each other on matters of mutual interest and seek each others sincere advice. When we make decisions on our own, we are more likely to make a mistake than when we consult other concerned people. The *shura* does not mean we discuss everything with everyone. The *shura* must be among the people who are concerned with the specific issue to be discussed.

It is also our responsibility to give advice in *shura* when asked. To give someone advice is also a kind of *'amanah,* a trust. If we are involved in a *shura,* we must keep to secrecy and regard it as the most important trust. We must not talk about it with unconcerned people, we must then give the issue our best consideration and offer our best advice.

> There are different forms of *shura.* In the *shura* of the family, we discuss family matters with the members of our family. In our community centers and *Masajid* we must discuss matters relating to the community. In our neighborhoods, cities and the country we must discuss matters which are the concern of our neighborhood, the   city and the country.
>
> Democracy is also one form of *shura.* Any form of *shura* is better than no *shura.* Every decision made through *shura* is blessed by Allah ﷻ and is less likely to be wrong. We must practice *shura* and participate in all forms of *shura* at every level in our family, community and society and help each group reach the best decision.

Al-Khulafa' Ar-Rashidun were elected by

shura of the Muslims. After the selection by the senior *Sahabah,* all people were invited to offer *bai'ah,* or the pledge of obedience to them.

The principle of *shura* required rulers to consult their subjects on important matters of common concern. The kings and rulers in ancient times ruled through their free will. Some of them, like the Pharaohs of Egypt, declared themselves gods. They did not see the need to consult others or follow their advice.

Seeking other people's advice in matters of policy is even more important for the rulers. One of their wrong decisions could affect the
lives of a large number of people. However, most of those in power often do not want to bind themselves to any rule or advice and want to exercise their power completely.

Islamic *Khilafah* established a new principle, the rule of law. The rule of law means that no one is above the law and rulers have a responsibility to rule according to the law of the land.

The pledge of obedience by the people to the *Khalifah* was conditional, Muslims would obey him if he obeyed Allah ﷻ and His Messenger ﷺ. Thus, the *'Ummah* would owe him no obedience if he did not follow the Qur'an and the *Sunnah.* The *Khulafa'* happily submitted themselves to the Qur'an and the *Sunnah* and invited everyone to participate in the *shura.*

These *Khulafa'* asked for the general *shura* on all important matters and the *shura* of special people on specific issues. There was a large number of non-Muslims in Muslim lands and there were many occasions to make a decision in matters which may affect them. There were many other matters in newly conquered territories where their ad-vice may be of crucial importance. Thus both the Muslims and the non-Muslims were part of the *shura* of the Islamic State.

The *Khilafah* was also a responsible form of government. People were free to question the *Khalifah* on any matter, be it of his personal life or state policy.

As 'Umar ﷺ spoke from the *minbar* (the pulpit) of the *Masjid an-Nabi* a woman stood up and corrected 'Umar ﷺ. 'Umar ﷺ was taken aback but realized his mistake.

'Umar ﷺ gratefully accepted her opinion and said, "The woman spoke the truth and 'Umar has made a mistake."

There was no concept of human rights in the ancient world. The idea of human rights means that all human beings, irrespective of their color, language, religion, and race, have certain rights. These rights must be respected by all. For example, all people have freedom to their religion, privacy, good family life, and legal protection. The idea of human rights is something new in the West, but Islam preached it from the very beginning. Islam grants human rights to all its citizens. The Qur'an gives a very long list of human rights to which every human being is entitled.

These *Al-Khulafa' Ar-Rashidun* followed Allah's commands and the *Sunnah* of Rasulullah ﷺ and gave all people under their rule human rights that no other people in the world possessed.

> The Islamic state became so famous for its tolerance and protection of human rights that even non-Muslims left their homes and rule of coreligionists to come and live in the Islamic State. The Islamic State protected the Jews from the intolerance of Christians and some Christian sects from the intolerance of other Christian sects.

Al-Khilafah Ar-Rashidah established another new concept in government, a welfare state. A welfare state is a new concept in the West but Islam introduced this idea and *Al-Khilafah Ar-Rashidah* established it in practice. The idea of welfare state is that the state is established for the welfare of the people and not for the comfort of its rulers. The welfare state must fulfill the basic needs of all its citizens such as food, shelter, education, and health.

As the financial situation of the Muslim State improved, it took more and more interest in the general well-being of all its citizens.

> 'Umar ﷺ once said, "The best ruler, in the sight of Allah, is he whose subjects are happy and contented and the worst ruler is he whose subjects are miserable."

The welfare state cannot function if the financial affairs of the state are not managed by the government in a responsible manner. In ancient times, the treasury of the state and all its resources belonged to the rulers and the kings and they could use it as they pleased. The Islamic *Bait ul-Mal* was not, however, the property of the *Khulafa'*, but a trust of the *'Ummah*. Even the *Khalifah* could not withdraw any money for his personal needs. They received small allowances which were fixed by the *Shura* Council.

Once 'Ali ﷺ saw his daughter wearing a necklace which she borrowed from the *Bait ul-Mal* for 'Id day. It made 'Ali ﷺ very angry and he made her return it immediately.

The *Bait ul-Mal* provided for the needs of all its needy citizens. First, during the rule of 'Umar ﷺ, children received stipends as they were weaned away from mother's milk. Some needy mothers forced their children before time to receive the help from *Bait ul-Mal*. When 'Umar ﷺ came to know about it he asked to change the rule and fixed the allowances for the children from the time of their birth.

Needy non-Muslims also were entitled to receive stipends from the *Bait ul-Mal*. Each *Khalifah* had shown special concern

> 'Abu Bakr ﷺ accepted this allowance reluctantly and it was so small that even his most basic needs were not met. He accepted it because he had no other source of income and the affairs of the state took all his time. At the time of his death he sold all his belongings and returned the money to the treasury.

for the non-Muslim subjects and advised their representatives to be always fair and just to them.

After the period of *Al-Khilafah Ar-Rashidah,* Muslim rulers continued to call themselves *Khulafa'* but they rarely practiced the principle of *shura.* They were not elected by the *'Ummah* but came to power either by force or by nomination of their ruling family or royal father. The Muslim *Khilafah* became a form of kingship.

In later Islamic history, though true *Khilafah* was never established, there have been many pious rulers and officials who followed the example of *Al-Khulafa' Ar-Rashidun* in their personal lives and upheld the principles of *Al-Khilafah Ar-Rashidah* in their government policies; such rulers and officials were always looked at with favor by the *'Ummah.*

All the Muslims believe our governments and individual lives must be based upon the principles which are shown to us by the Qur'an, the *Sunnah,* the example of the *Khulafa'* and other *Sahabah.* Most of the principles of the Islamic *Khilafah* are now accepted by every sensible government of the world. These principles are, in fact, for everyone and forever.

Words and Terms to Remember:

Bai'ah, citizen, democracy, human rights, pledge, welfare state

---

We Have Learned:

- *Al-Khilafah Ar-Rashidah* is regarded as the best period in the history of Islam.

- The *Khilafah* was based upon the principles of *shura,* constitutional rule, and a welfarestate.

- The *Khilafah* protected the human rights of all its citizens irrespective of religion, language, color and origin.

About the Author

Dr. Abdullah Ahsan

Dr. Abdullah Ahsan was born in former East Pakistan (Bangladesh) and educated at Quaid-i-Azam University, Islamabad, Pakistan, McGill University, Montreal, Canada, and the University of Michigan, Ann Arbor, Michigan, from where he received his Ph. D. in History. He has worked at the Washington-based International Institute of Islamic Thought, and the International Islamic University, Islamabad, Pakistan. Currently he is Professor of History at the International Islamic University, Kuala Lumpur, Malaysia.

Dr. Ahsan has published articles in the *American Journal of Islamic Social Sciences, Journal of the Institute of Muslim Minority Affairs*, and *Tawhid*. Other books by this author include:

OIC: Introduction to an Islamic Political Institution, published by the International Institute of Islamic Thought (U.S.A.)

Ummah or Nation: Identity Crisis in Contemporary Muslim Society, published by the Islamic Foundation (U.K.)